CW01043997

MIRACLE DOG
MIRACLE GOD

MIRACLE DOG MIRACLE GOD

WHAT GOD THE FATHER TAUGHT
ME ABOUT HIMSELF THROUGH
THE LOVE OF A DOG

JOHN MCCREEDY

authorHOUSE®

AuthorHouse™ UK Ltd.
1663 Liberty Drive
Bloomington, IN 47403 USA
www.authorhouse.co.uk
Phone: 0800.197.4150

© 2013 John McCreedy. All rights reserved.

No part of this book may be reproduced, stored in a retrieval system, or transmitted by any means without the written permission of the author.

Published by AuthorHouse 10/08/2013

ISBN: 978-1-4918-8037-1 (sc)
ISBN: 978-1-4918-8039-5 (hc)
ISBN: 978-1-4918-8038-8 (e)

Any people depicted in stock imagery provided by Thinkstock are models, and such images are being used for illustrative purposes only. Certain stock imagery © Thinkstock.

This book is printed on acid-free paper.

Because of the dynamic nature of the Internet, any web addresses or links contained in this book may have changed since publication and may no longer be valid. The views expressed in this work are solely those of the author and do not necessarily reflect the views of the publisher, and the publisher hereby disclaims any responsibility for them.

TABLE OF CONTENTS

FOREWORD

By Joy Patterson

I have loved dogs from I was very young, so, you can imagine my delight when Pastor John McCreedy told me he had written a book about Snowbell, their lovely dog in Romania, and how he had learned so much from that particular creature. I was delighted, humbled and privileged to be allowed to read this book and I soon had difficulty in leaving it down. For, not only were Snowbell's adventures so interesting, the lessons learned from this dog were tremendous. How encouraging and instructive it was to my own heart. In the past, I have lifted down many new Christian books in shops, only to be disappointed that they contained so little of God's precious Word and some of them weren't even interesting to read. But not so with this volume, and in fact, I told him afterwards that this was the best book I have read in many, many years.

My family and I have known Pastor John McCreedy for a number of years. He is one who radiates the spirit of Christian love and he is an "example of the believers in word, in conversation, in charity, in faith, in purity." (I Timothy 4:12b) His talents are dedicated to the service of his Lord and Saviour, and whether in his capacity as an assistant Pastor in the Whitewell Metropolitan Tabernacle in Belfast, as writer of the widely read "Coffee Break" on the church's website, or as an author, his chief objective is to glorify God, to point sinners to the Lord Jesus Christ for salvation and to encourage the people of God. For almost a decade, Pastor John and his wife and godly help-meet, Louise, had a tremendous missionary work in Romania, not only looking after a number of children in what was known as "The Children's House", but also pastoring a church and looking after the poor in the village in practical terms. That work still bears fruit today, as they hear of the children, now young men and women, going to university and doing well, but above all, following the Lord Jesus Christ, Whom they came to know and love under the ministry and care of these two dedicated missionaries.

Snowbell will have you laughing and will also bring tears to your eyes. This was indeed a extraordinary dog used by the Lord for His special purpose. I heartily commend this book to a wide readership. May it contain a word in season for many and may it be used to bring glory to God, and to extend Christ's Kingdom in Northern Ireland and throughout the world. Joy Patterson.

ACKNOWLEDGEMENTS

I would like to begin by dedicating this book to my faithful wife Louise, known to the children in Romania as "Mama Louise". Words could never do justice to her commitment to me and to our ministry in Romania. I wish to thank, too, my former secretary Lacramioara and the staff and children of the Children's House, Carani, Romania, for the role they have played in this remarkable story. I am much indebted also to James and Joy Patterson and Samuel and Sadie Jamison for showing my wife Louise and I the love of God following our return from Romania. It would be almost impossible to describe how these saints helped restore us following our missionary endeavours.

I further wish to express my gratitude to my good friend Natalie Gregory, ("Mrs E") for her continual encouragement and determination to see me publish this book. Without this encouragement, I'm not sure if I would have ever finished this manuscript.

Finally, I owe a massive thank you to my proof reader Jackie Davidson for faithfully proofing every chapter and to Lorna Hamilton for painting a beautiful portrait of Snowbell which I have used as the front cover of the book. All of the above mentioned are an inspiration to me and I thank God for them every day.

PREFACE

A MIRACULOUS INTERVENTION

("And without a parable spake he not to them"
Matthew 13:34).

The following is a remarkable tale of the impact a special dog named Snowbell made upon my life, while serving as a missionary in Romania along with my wife Louise. It's a story of achievement mixed with sadness and recalls how love triumphs over hatred and prejudice. A true story, throughout this book, many of Snowbell's wonderful qualities are highlighted, as are the beautiful attributes of God; hence the title "Miracle Dog, Miracle God". Primarily the book is about what God the Father taught me about Himself through the love of a dog but, before reading it, let me expand on how we first came to be in Romania, then enlighten the reader further on how this remarkable dog was used to bring enormous healing to our hearts.

Crazy as that may sound Snowbell, a dog we purchased a short time before our return to Ireland in 2008, was truly a Godsend to both us and our home. I and my wife Louise had experienced some major disillusionment during our formative years in the eastern European country, but once this little puppy entered the grounds of our abode the entire atmosphere changed. His nature and mannerisms were at times heavenly, a dog with an ability to touch the heart of a human like no one else could. He was able to help us appreciate again the simple things in life. Ben Williams states "There is no psychiatrist in the world like a puppy licking your face".

I would lose count of how many times Snowbell not only licked my face, but also my wounds.

Observe the similarity in each short love story about Snowbell and the love story known as the gospel of Jesus Christ. Read in parable-like fashion how, due to his amazing love, a little Romanian-born dog totally transformed the life of someone who for many years detested dogs—me. Then compare this with how God's Son can equally transform the lives of millions through the simplicity of the gift of love.

Snowbell's love was irresistible, constant and unfailing. His love was totally unconditional. This amazing dog soothed our pain and got our lives back on track at just the right time. Looking back, his arrival was nothing short of a miraculous intervention.

INTRODUCTION

AN INCONVENIENT CALL

"Verily I say unto you, there is no man that has left house or
brethren, or sister, or father, or mother or wife, or children,
or lands, for my sake and the gospels, but he shall receive an
hundred fold, now in this time, houses and brethren, sisters
and mothers and children and lands, **with persecutions,** and
in the world to come eternal life" (Mark 10:29-30).

GOD'S CALL IS NOT ALWAYS A CONVENIENT CALL.

A new millennium had dawned and expectations were high. The
year 2000 was an exciting time to be alive and keeping up with
rapid advances in technology appeared to be uppermost in the
minds of an increasingly high-tech generation. Facebook, Twitter and the
ipad were relatively unheard of, but they were about to go global. It was
a period when real change was blowing across the world, yet no more so
than in our own lives.

My wife Louise and I were seeking confirmation regarding a move to
the mission-field and we were about to get it in dramatic fashion. The
location in question was a little village called Carani in Western Romania
which sheltered and schooled orphan children at our church-sponsored
home there. The sheer thought of such change in our lives was terrifying,
especially where I was concerned. The only thing I knew about Romania

was that it managed to produce a talented tennis player named IIie Nastase, whose comical antics at the Wimbledon tennis tournament in London are still legendary.

Nastase was undoubtedly an exceptional talent, a sporting character if ever there was one, but his on-court pranks often meant he didn't win as much as he should have. I was aware also of the equally famous Romanian sportswoman, Nadia Comaneci, the first gymnast ever to score a perfect 10.0 at the 1981 Olympic Games at the tender age of just 14. Otherwise, I knew very little about the Balkan-based country and, frankly, I didn't want to go there. The idea of being wrenched away from my family, friends and normal form of employment to a struggling foreign country wasn't exactly appealing, particularly when things were becoming so interesting at home. Rather than "move with the times", it was clear we would be taking a step "back in time" by going to Romania.

I was about to learn, however, that God's call is not always a convenient call. It calls us to where He wants us to be and not to where we choose for ourselves.

I have heard God's call on several occasions over the years. Some have been small instructions, others larger—none more so than Romania—yet all of them were tests of my own willingness and devotion towards the cause of Christ. Some I have willingly accepted and others have proven much more difficult for me to surrender to. Back in the year 2000, I was enjoying life and couldn't ever have imagined myself involved in anything other than what I was currently doing. Prior to this experience, everything I had worked for during 15 years in journalism seemed to be coming to fruition.

Things had progressed nicely for me in my career as a radio and television presenter in Northern Ireland and I was literally fulfilling my lifelong dream of presenting news and sport on TV. Doors of opportunity appeared to be opening up for me in broadcasting and naturally I was excited. Who wouldn't be when my life appeared to be going according to my own plan! Journalism had become a way of life to me; the friends and colleagues I had made were special people I would deeply miss if I left. Nevertheless, God has a way of speaking to our hearts and turning us towards the work of His kingdom when we least expect it; yes, even at the most inconvenient times. Such experiences are known as "God's divine interruptions". For a number of years I had written hundreds of articles, served my time presenting packages for both radio and television programmes and was convinced it was my time to shine, but amazingly my whole personality, aspirations and dreams seem to change. It was like I had undergone heart surgery in the most spiritual sense, of course. All of a sudden I desired the ministry more than the buzz of "breaking" daily stories. One of those divine interruptions was about to visit my own life, something I found hard to come to terms with.

From having my heart set on working for secular media, I now had an overwhelming desire to spread the good news of the gospel. I had become immensely conscious of a statement a former editor of a newspaper had made to me during my first week with the paper. He told me: "Today's news is tomorrow's fish and chips packet" and how true that remark became. No sooner had I written one story than the next one was required and within a few days my little masterpiece was in the bin and confined to history. As I considered this reality, it was becoming more apparent to me that God's Word is not so. Jesus made it clear that "heaven and earth shall pass away, but my word shall never pass away" (Luke 21:23). Isaiah also stated "The grass withers, the flower fades; but the word of our God will stand forever (Isaiah 40:8). Although I desperately wanted to write and preach about this kind of constancy, the call of God still frightened me senseless.

In the Old Testament Samuel brought news from God that the people didn't always want to hear. Samuel's call wasn't exactly an appealing one. Called out of his comfort zone, the scripture also tells us that God stood by Samuel the rest of his life. When we follow God's call we can be certain that God will follow us. His step into the unknown will always require us to demonstrate courage and faith, but the Lord will always provide for us. Frederick Buechner says "The place God calls you to, is the place where your gladness and the world's great hunger meet".

Touching down for the very first time in Timisoara in the year 2000, it was clear that there was great hunger, not just physically amongst the poor, but spiritual hunger, too. As we began to experience a new life across many waters, we were totally unaware of just how much Romania would prove a major turning point in our lives. Upon arrival, I recall being immensely conscious of the feel of the place. Not a nice feel, mind you, but a needy one. The lonely and helpless looks of the children were heart-wrenching to observe. Total hopelessness decorated their eyes. No one could have failed to have been untouched by their situations and shocking stories. From the outside they may have appeared normal, but inside you could tell they were screaming. Remember this was a time when Romanian orphanages were packed with children, many of whom were left abandoned by their parents. Television documentaries had been broadcast throughout the world revealing the dreadful plight of these infants, lots of whom were crammed into rooms and left to fend for themselves. They say the "need is not always the call", nevertheless, regarding the biggest demand of our own lives, the need proved to be very much the call. Compassion set in and, by God's grace, commitment followed. A peace came and everything felt just right. Having observed, at close proximity, both poverty and oppression, especially amongst children, it was a mission neither of us in the end could refuse; I knew in my heart that Romania was calling me even if I wasn't calling for Romania. For months I had fought against the idea of a new life in this part of Europe, refusing to even mention the word Romania in my prayers in case God heard me, but street children were running wild everywhere and illegal international adoption and human trafficking of them was a regular occurrence back then. We could either turn a blind eye to this, or do something positive about it. In the end, we heard God's bell ring and responded. I became convinced it was my duty to answer this invitation. My spirit responded to God's higher purpose for my life. Nothing seemed logical, yet God still managed to drag us both out of our comfort zone. Methodist minister George Irvine once stated "If it's loving, if it's just, if it promotes right relationships, and if it scares the hell out of you, it just might be a call from God".

We had chosen to respond to a call we were frightened of. We would eventually venture to a strange land with more than a little trepidation; a land hungry and in great want, yet throughout our incredible journey we felt a joy in the midst of daily trial and remarkably God met every need. We would learn how God's call should never be construed as a job. My experiences would ultimately teach me many lessons; not least that God's call is not always appealing, or indeed convenient. We don't always appreciate such interruptions in our lives and I, for one, was no exception.

At one point, Romania was the last place on earth I wanted to go to, but then I wasn't the first person to shy away from the will of God. Think of the story of Jonah in the Old Testament—a man who knew in his heart that he was to go to the city of Nineveh to preach, yet instead decided to try and run away from the call of God, which greater men than he had tried before to do and failed. While aboard the ship a mighty storm came and suddenly Jonah found himself overboard and inside the belly of a great fish which held him captive for three days and three nights before finally releasing him unto the shore. Jonah, as before, was then given the very same instruction by the Lord to go to the lost city of Nineveh and preach against it.

Sometimes it's a great deal easier to do that which God gives us to do, no matter how hard it is, than to face the responsibilities of not doing it. And so Jonah finally obeyed the Lord.

Often we are reluctant to respond to the call of God in our lives. In the ancient days of Eli and Samuel, the word of the Lord was rare and visions were scarce. God speaks to us, but we are too busy and even frightened to respond to God's call as it usually proves inconvenient for us and our families. Pastors are often asked "How do I know I am in the will of God?" The will of God is an attitude, not a place. If we are to hear from God, we need to listen to God before making any radical change in our lives.

Nevertheless, in my experience, answering God's call requires caution as much as boldness. For example, when someone embraces the call of God too quickly and without reservation, it's quite normal for them to feel the promptings of God and be filled with enthusiasm. More often than not, however, God's assignment for our lives is so challenging that it leaves us overawed, in the same way I was when Romania came knocking upon the door. There's nothing wrong with caution. Caution is not cowardice! Caution is both biblical and sensible. If you receive what God was unwilling to give, it may prove a most painful experience. Oswald Chambers writes "Doubt is not always a sign that a man is wrong; it may be a sign that he is thinking". Even Jesus advised caution before starting any new project stating "For which of you, intending to build a tower, sits not down first and counts the cost whether or not he have sufficient to finish it?" (Luke 14:28).

Enthusiasm and a kind heart is not enough when it comes to the call of God. The right thing at the wrong time ultimately becomes the wrong thing. Waiting until God makes it impossible for us to say no is a better option. I still recall how my wife and I were seeking God for years, not months, prior to our Romanian call. We had fasted, prayed and heard from God, but all of this was vital to ultimately know His presence would be with us when we left the shores of Ireland. We had faith in God's timing.

Throughout the Bible we read of many servants of God with a call on their lives, many of whom literally had to be cornered into taking up their vocation. Lots of people do not want to obey such a request, something which is not entirely surprising or new. From Genesis to Revelation we read of great men such as Moses, Jeremiah, Isaiah, Gideon, David and in the New Testament the apostle Paul all of whom had trouble obeying the purpose of God for their lives. These men were terrified about answering God's call because they didn't feel worthy of such a task. When we also reach this same place of respect and humility, God may just be ready to use us.

In the first book of Corinthians Paul highlights the real qualifications required for ministers of God. Firstly he announces that he was not called by men, but by God. He explains how his call was as an apostle of Jesus Christ through the will of God (1 Cor 1:1). Later he adds "For ye see your calling, brethren, how that not many wise men after the flesh, not many noble, are called: but God hath chosen the foolish things of the world to confound the wise; and God hath chosen the weak things of the world to confound the things that are mighty; and base things of the world and things which are despised, hath God chosen, yea and things which are not, to bring to nought things that are; that no flesh should glory in His presence" (I Corinthians 1-26-31).

Doing God's will in His time is never easy, but if we surrender to His greater purpose for our lives, He gives us grace sufficient for the task ahead. "When we learn to say a deep, passionate yes to the things that really matter, then peace begins to settle onto our lives like golden sunlight sifting to a forest floor", said Thomas Kinkade.

Provision is only certain when you reach the place of your assignment. It isn't easy to get up and leave the thing we are content to do for that which is more necessary, but that's often how God interrupts our lives. He rings the bell when we least expect it and the power of obedience has a way of making things possible which previously seemed impossible. Martin Luther King Jnr once stated "Faith is taking the first step, even when we don't see the whole staircase". This is how we felt as we arrived in Romania. Answering God's call takes courage, but it's the right thing to do and the Lord honours such courage. Men may not necessarily appreciate or agree with what you do; they may not even understand it, but if it's the will of the Father for your life, you can be certain God will mark it in heaven.

PROLOGUE

HIT BY A HURRICANE

("Blessed are ye when men shall revile you and persecute you
and say all manner of evil against you falsely for my name's
sake. Rejoice and be exceedingly glad for great is your reward
in heaven. For so persecuted they the prophets which were
before you" (Matthew 5:18, 19).

IN THE MIDST OF DARKNESS NEW DREAMS CAN STILL SURFACE.

Following our official arrival in 2001, I didn't have long to wait to encounter our first major storm in Romania. Enjoying a quite tropical day, I noticed dark clouds in the distance; clouds which rapidly increased in size while the wind gathered speed in an unusual way. Then, like a bolt from the blue, it hit us; what felt like a mini tornado swept right through the entire village knocking over everything in its path, including me. While at university in America during the 1980's I recall getting caught up in a violent storm in Kansas City, but this was by far the most ferocious wind storm I'd ever encountered. I was trapped at the gate and the gusts were so strong I couldn't get back to the door of the house. I felt like Judy Garland in the Wizard of Oz. There was dust everywhere, especially in my eyes and, to make matters worse the heavens opened. Huge hail stones, the size of golf balls, beat upon my head and it was a relief to finally make it back to the house. Even then the wind was so strong I was convinced the house was going to fall down around us and it was several hours before calm was completely restored to the village. I dared to go back outside only to witness incredible devastation all around me. Tables, chairs and fences were destroyed, while some neighbours had their roofs blown off and others had their properties demolished. I'd never seen anything like it. A strong wind continued to blow into my face, but nowhere near as powerful as the earlier one that had practically destroyed the village. Of course, long after the last winds and waves of any hurricane season have blown inland, the storm continues its anger, before eventually petering out. There are always aftershocks, strong gusts, thunder and lightning and heavy rain, not to mention the dreadful economic consequences of such a storm. Hurricanes don't normally fully end until they lose power and losing power means being replaced by more milder, tolerant weather systems.

The same principle applies to the corrupt regimes of our world. None of these establishments disappear without an almighty fight and this was certainly true of Nicolae Ceausescu's old Romania. Unfortunately we had arrived at the tail end of this hurricane-like totalitarian system and we felt the full force of its brutal backlash. Incidents such as the ones which used to take place under the rule of the notorious dictator Ceausescu back in the bad old days of the 1980's, although supposedly a thing of the past, were clearly still occurring in this country. During the 1989 revolution, which finally brought Ceausescu's authority to an end, no fewer than 5,000 people were killed, particularly in Timisoara, a city situated not far from where our home now stood. I still recollect how my translator took me into the city to show me the bullet holes from over a decade before, which were still clearly visible on a wall directly adjacent to a McDonald's fast food outlet. In addition to the 5,000 people killed during 1989, there were possibly thousands of deaths per year during the entire 1980's in Romania from deprivations caused by an unnecessary austerity programme. Tens of thousands more lives were ruined during Ceausescu's barbaric reign. The economy was at an all-time low, not to mention the morale of the Romanian people. The most appalling legacy left by this tyrant, however, was the countless filthy, neglected children rescued from Romanian orphanages and institutions Ceausescu claimed did not exist. Ceausescu's policies over the previous decades had caused a truly horrific state of affairs for Romanian children. His laws banning birth-control, displacing entire populations and pursuing industrial growth led simultaneously to extreme poverty, the breakup of traditional family structures and a sharp increase in child abandonment. By 1990 there were apparently 170,000 children living in over 700 institutions. After his death, the deplorable conditions of these institutions were exposed and the world immediately responded, leading to many questionable adoptions of thousands of Romanian orphans. Even prior to our arrival Communist red tape was everywhere despite the fact that communism itself was supposedly dead. I would switch on the news and hear about the new Romania now ready for EU membership but, in truth, we were all still living in the old Romania. The paper work was colossal. One almost required a government stamp to visit the toilet. I remember one day having to sign my name hundreds of times just to allow one of our children to attend school kindergarten. I felt like David Beckham at an international book launch. Although you would never have guessed, this was a period when Romania was supposed to be "getting its house in order" with regard to potential entry into the EU.

Instead, in those early days, we were reliably informed our home was constantly bugged and, being interrogated in side rooms at the airport or other places where officialdom was constant, was still commonplace. Frequently I would have to fly to another country just to post an important letter on behalf of our home as it would never make its intended destination if posted in Romania. Infamous dictator Ceausescu may no longer have been alive, having been executed almost 20 years previously, but his influence was everywhere. You could literally smell the oppression in the air. I was shocked one day when a leading European politician refused to continue a phone call with me, telling me, "Mr McCreedy, they (secret police) are listening to us right now and if you want to continue this correspondence call me from another country and we will talk more". Growing up during Ceausescu's time in power people in Romania carried around a terrible certainty that many of their friends and even family members were informers for the dreaded Securitate secret police. According to the Securitate's own archives, an estimated 750,000 people out of a population of 23 million collaborated, meaning around one in 30 were on the payroll of Ceausecu. Now I was being told that little had changed, something I was becoming all too aware of. From that point on, phone calls, emails and text messages were kept very general as it suddenly dawned on me that very little in Romania was private. It also became obvious that despite reports to the contrary, Romania was still operating with a deeply rooted communist mind-set. Sometimes our minds are harder to change than our hearts. The mind or brain has the capacity to either think good thoughts or corrupt thoughts. Jesus said "Let this mind be in you, which was also in Christ Jesus" (Philippians 2:5).

In the same way Northern Ireland is taking generations to rid itself of the mind-set of religious bigotry and hatred, so, too, it became clear that Romania would not itself be able to shake off the mind-set of communism in an instant. Corruption was still omnipresent at every level of society. It was widespread in the healthcare sector which offered derisory salaries and pitifully low pensions. I regularly recall seeing patients at the hospitals with little envelopes for every member of staff they encountered; for the receptionists, the nurses and doctors. Exposed on the hospital trolley these poor souls had a fistful of lei for the specialist who was about to put them to sleep. Corruption was apparent in schools, in the police, in commerce, in the tax office, in public exams, and most importantly in politics. The judicial system in particular was a shambles and a total farce. Many lies were told about people, including ourselves, if they were seen as a threat to the Romanian authorities. Add to this the fact that the scourge of forbidden international adoptions had returned to Romania's garden at the beginning of the new millennium, a procedure which resulted in a broadside from the EU warning the Romanian government that if such adoptions didn't cease, Romania's place in the EU would ultimately be jeopardised. Thousands of Romanian orphans were 'adopted' by foreign families or simply smuggled out to unknown destinations between the fall of the communist regime in 1989 and the passing of a new law on adoption in June 1995. However, despite being embarrassed by the worldwide image that Romanian children were for sale, the governments' moratorium on adoptions back in 1991 was clearly not working. Amendments to the adoption laws had allowed courts at local level to handle the cases, which had resulted in another rash of adoptions and allegedly inspired new networks of unauthorised middlemen who were being paid to match cash-carrying foreigners with desperate parents and corrupt court officials. Sadly the new millennium appeared to be starting in exactly the same way as the latter part of the old millennium had ended. Baby smuggling and illegal payments to local authorities were on the rise, although no reliable estimates could ever be established. Unsurprisingly, however, those words appeared to fall on deaf ears.

During my time in Romania I flew thousands of miles in search of justice for children. I attended the European Parliament on several occasions in both Brussels and Strasbourg in order to highlight the shocking cases of child abuse and corruption which were taking place as a result of illegal international adoption in Romania. This entailed challenging the Romanian and European legal system at the very highest level of the Supreme Court itself by our organisation, but obtaining a positive outcome in the Romanian courts proved very difficult, not to mention how our decision to oppose this practice in general in Romania would eventually prove costly, life-changing and even damaging to our health. I still recall the awful frequent experiences of being sneered at in court rooms, then searched and detained at airports. Whether or not it was personal I still don't know, but it felt like it. The rooms at airports were often incredibly hot, with someone sitting glaring at me. In a corner, another person was busy leafing through paperwork. I would just sit there, often beside some other poor foreign traveller, always left to wait in trepidation. Despite the searing temperatures, such detention would sometimes last for hours before being told "You can go".'

I was forever conscious, too, of being tailed regularly by what I presumed were Secret Police. The so-called new transparency which was supposed to have replaced Ceausescu's period of persecution was nowhere to be found. That initial sense of excitement and faith we had felt at the beginning of a new millennium was about to be replaced by both genuine fear and feelings of utter despair. At times we were verbally abused, totally ostracised, bitterly betrayed by some of the legal teams we employed to represent us, had our reputations destroyed both in Romania and in Ireland and all because we sought to protect the best interests of children. Regularly I would ask myself the question "how did we get into this mess?"

Looking back, our arrival in Romania was like landing in hell; we had arrived in the darkest place I can ever recall. We were trapped in a spiritual warzone, unlike anything we'd ever encountered. Jesus said in the New Testament "Blessed are ye when men shall revile you and persecute you and say all manner of evil against you falsely for my name's sake. Rejoice and be exceedingly glad for great is your reward in heaven. For so persecuted they the prophets which were before you" (Matthew 5:18, 19). Never before had these words related so much to my own life. From the very outset, we were constantly at odds with the local authorities regarding the apathy which seemed to exist regarding normal child protection procedures. It seemed we could do nothing to please the authorities and for the next several years persecution visited our door in unimaginable ways. This ranged from threats, to slander, to isolation and humiliation and left us feeling exhausted and downcast in spirit. Don't expect the devil to roll out a red carpet when you take up God's commission. He will oppose everything you try to do, particularly in nations with a history of spiritual repression.

Following two bitterly fought court battles in search of justice for our home and the children, both of which lasted over 5 years, Romania would ultimately prove a crushing blow to my gullible views about life in general. Perhaps I naively assumed this country would applaud our efforts to help take care of their orphan children; instead, the same nation punished us severely. As John Betjeman wrote "Childhood is measured out by sounds, sights and smells, before the darkness of reason grows". Suddenly everything I'd ever trusted in during childhood simply didn't exist anymore; justice, truth and general compassion, which previously I had believed prevailed in the world, disintegrated before my very eyes. Call me naïve, but this wasn't what I imagined life would serve me. On reflection it was a wake-up call very much required. Growing up I was quite sheltered. I viewed the world through "rose coloured spectacles" and saw it as almost perfect at times, but this is far from true. God may have created a beautiful world, but through sinfulness, greed and corruption, man has made it an ugly place to live in. Darkness, pain and injustice does arrive at our doorstep like any unwanted imposter especially when we least expect it.

Not only do both the Old and New Testaments remind us of this possibility, they also reveal in great detail how major Bible characters themselves were not immune to injustice and suffering. God never promised His children a carefree existence, especially those who seek to serve Him. Seasons of exceptional trouble do come; how we handle these seasons is what's important. Paul wrote "yea, and all that shall live godly in Christ Jesus shall suffer persecution" (2 Timothy 3:12). This persecution, whether psychological, which was the case in Romania, or physical, like in Iraq, Afghanistan, Syria, China and North Korea, is well documented throughout the scriptures. In the Old Testament David cried, "How long shall I take counsel in my soul having sorrows in my heart daily? How long shall my enemy be exalted over me?" (Psalm 13:2).

Nevertheless the same David managed to outlast the bitter king Saul and one day he became King of Israel. David even had the misfortune of having his entire village ransacked by the Amalekites and his wives and goods stolen, but later he recovered everything from his enemies. Why do such calamities gate-crash our lives in the first place? The apostle Paul says "For we wrestle not against flesh and blood, but against principalities, against the rulers of the darkness of this world, against spiritual wickedness in high places" (Ephesians 6:12). The term "high places" is significant. Some Bible translations refer to this expression as meaning "wicked spirits operating in the spirit realm", while others suggest the text relates to the "higher echelons of the seat of secular government". In other words when ordinary men and women challenge global judicial powers, they should expect a fierce backlash of spiritual wickedness against them. This was my experience in those early days in Romania. Without question the decision to go there and challenge their judicial system became a life-changing experience destined to permanently shape my future.

Following the 9/11 disaster at the World Trade Centre in 2001, an editorial in the New York Times read "It was one of those moments in which history splits and we define the world as "before" and "after". Of course, from Belfast to Beijing, millions captured live on their television sets the sight of the worst terrorist attack in history. How disturbing it must have proven to experience this tragedy and to watch this scene develop right there on the streets of New York. America would never be the same again; nor our world. People's faith in their nation, government, security and yes, even in God, appeared to be completely shattered. Darkness had descended upon mankind unlike anything previously felt. A season of exceptional trouble had ruthlessly invaded our planet. Yet following 9/11, I knew instantly that my life was undergoing a plane crash of its own. My faith in God and in human decency was also about to be strongly challenged. I too was in the midst of a "before" and "after" occurrence, which even today many years later has left its mark upon my life.

Nevertheless new dreams can still surface. In our world, every storm has an end and every night brings a new day. Like that powerful yet brief mini tornado that swept through our village, storms come and go; what's important is to trust those you love and never give up. A host of storms are raging around the world today, storms of unemployment, divorce, bankruptcy, depression, ill-health and economic recession. We must never give up hope, however, for God's plan for your life will not be stopped by a storm. The battle is not ours, it's the Lord's. When He is with us, when He is working out the purposes of our lives, we experience beauty for ashes in the most amazing ways. No tempest, no matter how ferocious, can prevent God's will being accomplished in our lives.

Following our own battles in Romania, broken dreams were all around me. Many times I recall being desperate to leave, but I knew I had to stay. Barely clinging on, I urgently required something wonderful, even supernatural to take place; something to help get me through the next few, difficult years which lay in front of us—something I never would have imagined, of course, not even in my wildest dreams—the arrival of a little Labrador.

CHAPTER ONE

───────※───────

A GIFT FROM GOD

"Thanks be unto God for His unspeakable gift"
(2 Corinthians 9:15).

LESSON 1—APPRECIATE GOD'S GIFT TO OUR LIVES.

Never in my life had I any wish to own a pet, especially a dog. In fact, to say I "hated dogs" would certainly not be an exaggeration. Our family were not brought up with animals, I didn't like the smell of them and I certainly couldn't have imagined owning one. Thankfully, however, my parents had no interest in pets which suited me just fine.

None of the above-mentioned reservations are why I actually detested dogs. The reason was much more personal. During my youth, I was a junior international athlete specialising in middle distance running. My training would take me to various parklands and places of recreation where I would regularly be chased by a multitude of these barking creatures. The dogs would continually try to bite me on the legs and took no notice of the fact that I was shouting frantically, "Go away, I'm a junior international athlete, you know!" Truly I not only loathed them, I was scared stiff of them and was convinced that this would be my attitude towards dogs as long as I lived.

Life, however, has a beautiful way of surprising us. One day, well over 20 years later, shortly after our arrival in Romania, I was introduced to Snowbell, a beautiful little Labrador. At that time my wife Louise lovingly looked after our forty one orphan children and, persuaded by many of these well-meaning, yet manipulative kids, she suddenly decided that it would be a good idea to invest in a dog for the children to play with. I was keen to point out to her and the children just why I thought it wouldn't be such a good idea to purchase one, but to no avail. There's an old saying: "you don't pick your dog, it picks you!" I now know that's absolutely true.

I well recall that first day when Snowbell arrived at our home. My wife had taken the children into the Romanian city of Timisoara for their normal Saturday excursion, but this particular week they had hatched a plan, one I was totally unaware of. They had decided to go to a shopping centre which had just opened a brand new dog store. When they arrived two dogs were in the small, made-up window. One was tiny, cuddly, white as snow and, of course, his eyes were saying "pick me, pick me please!" He was certainly intriguing as a puppy and, of course, he wasn't the only one saying pick me, please!! His little mate was also anxious to be selected that day. Certainly the children were all in unison regarding their new pending acquisition. With crowds of people thronging the shop deliberating whether or not to purchase the adorable little puppies, Mama finally caved in and bought one of them. "How will I explain to Pastor John" she excitedly exclaimed, as the bus drove them away with our new canine friend. The children just laughed and replied: "You'll think of something, Mama!"

Once they had returned home, explaining wasn't as easy as they had imagined. I was incensed at the news, immediately disowning him, of course. "He's not my dog, he's yours and the kids", I protested. "That's okay", said my wife, trying to pacify me. She obviously knew what I did not know, namely, that once the puppy made it through the door all would be well. And so it proved. It was love at first sight for all of us. Despite piddling on our newly completed summer balcony during his first week, not to mention destroying the front seats of my car on more than one occasion, no matter how hard I tried not to love this pet, in the end he would teach me a valuable lesson. Snowbell loved me in a way that I had never previously felt and through his show of affection I would eventually come to love him. The last thing I considered which might provide healing in my life at that moment was a dog. The huge prejudice I had built up over the years had separated me so much from dogs and from other animals, it would have proved a bridge too far for me to cross, or so I thought! Yet lovingly and patiently, this beautiful dog appeared to nurse us back to full health; moreover he restored in both of us that most important ingredient called love. Somebody told me that dogs are good for your stress levels and blood pressure. I think it's true. Dogs are such great stress reducers. Silly as it sounds, playing with Snowbell would ultimately become a most therapeutic form of activity not only for the children, but also for Louise and me. The stress of the Romanian encounters we had experienced prior to his timely arrival finally seemed to disperse a little. For the first time in a long while we started to afford ourselves some welcome light relief and I even began to like myself better as a person. He may have been just a puppy, yet hope sprang eternal following Snowbell's arrival at our house. The love and happiness this dog generated calmed me down, chilled me out and made me much mellower. Whoever said you can't buy happiness forgot to include Snowbell.

This little dog would eventually grow up to spread joy not just throughout our home, but throughout the entire village of Carani where we lived. Carani was a small rural community in Western Romania with around a thousand people in it. It was closely knit, but those who lived there were undemanding, friendly and the majority of them had animals of some kind. There were just a couple of shops in this humble little village which was quite remote and far removed from the bustle of the nearest city Timisoara, situated almost 30 kilometres away. Eventually nearly everyone in Carani would come to know Snowbell, if not by sight, then by the sound of his bark. They would readily identify with this placid and radiant pet and many even came to love him almost as much as we did. His arrival left all of our lives utterly altered in ways we could not believe. Back then he was just a puppy to me and I had no indication of just how remarkable this dog really was; I hadn't a clue as to how much he would change our lives. His birth had been a great gift to me, but I still hadn't really grasped that. To me he was just a dog and I didn't appreciate him at all!

In the same way, the majority of the children were too young to comprehend that just as Snowbell became a great gift in my life, the Children's House was equally a phenomenal gift which God had sent into their own troubled lives. This home was also a gift to Romania as a nation, not just to the children of the nation, but you wouldn't have thought so due to the hostile manner in which we were first received. Romania was a beautiful country, with many beautiful people, many of whom are still my friends today, but it was constantly a difficult one to reside in. Nevertheless, we had come as friends and helpers of Romanians, not only in financial terms, but also practically. No stone had been left unturned in terms of the excellence of the building and finishing of this home. The home was built at an eventual cost of well in excess of 500,000 euros thanks to the generosity of the members of the Metropolitan Tabernacle in Belfast, many of whom helped construct the home with their very own hands. It was a children's paradise compared to some of the other repulsive Romanian state orphanages we witnessed. The smell of these places was disgusting, while children were often crammed in like sardines. I once encountered what looked like a hundred children crammed into one single room, a sight I will never forget. On the contrary, the Children's House, Carani, was like an oasis and the care the children received was of the highest standard. Not all of them were orphaned, but all of them were homeless and needed a roof over their heads. Alternatively they received a place to live beyond their wildest imaginations for without exaggeration the Children's House, Carani, was like a palace and was viewed even by the Timisoara authorities as one of the top show homes in Romania, certainly in terms of its quality of facilities and cleanliness. The children fortunate enough to be selected to live there went from having little or no food to having their own cooks, they went from having either no bed or a poor bed to a room of their own with blankets washed and replaced daily. They had their own cleaners, a nurse on site and supervisors to educate them. Their entire education was paid for and in the afternoons they had private tutors to help them with their homeworks, teaching them the English language. They had their own bus driver who took them to and from school and on day trips with Louise every Saturday. The children loved their state-of-the art games room with television and amusements which other homes could only dream of. Despite the fact that they lived in an isolated part of the world, these children had been chosen by God to receive the greatest of blessings. Many of them were babies when they arrived, but they possessed so much potential and the Children's House was the perfect place for such potential to blossom. We constantly reminded the children that it was due to the grace of God and gift of God alone how they had been singled out to receive His favour and, although initially they couldn't fully appreciate this, as time progressed, they would come to understand it and consequently make a great impact on my own life. In the end I think I learned more from them than they learned from me. Like everyone else, of course, they just adored Snowbell, who was another incredible gift to their young lives. As the children told me the story of Snowbell as a puppy in that little shop window, I couldn't help but recall the birth of Christ. Born in Bethlehem in humble circumstances, He was worshipped and adored by many onlookers; a baby, yes, but one with an awesome mission in life. The Bible says of this town: "But you, Bethlehem Ephratah, though you are little among the thousands of Judah, yet out of you shall come forth unto me that is ruler in Israel, whose goings forth have been from old, from everlasting" (Micah 5:2).

Bethlehem is situated five and half miles from Jerusalem yet no town has such a glorious history of exalted status. Traditionally this city has personified great hope in the minds of humankind. Its historic and sacred meaning shines like a guiding star in our consciences. In terms of the major cities of the world Bethlehem is a backwater, but it's still the location God chose for the birth of His Son. It would be approximately 750 years following Isaiah's prophecy concerning the coming Messiah when an angel would speak directly, not to royalty or the awaiting multitudes, but to a lowly peasant woman named Mary, who was given the extraordinary news that she had been chosen to give birth to the Saviour of the world. Her husband Joseph was the village carpenter and, when told of Mary's pregnancy, Joseph obviously assumed an illicit relationship and moved to quietly dissolve the engagement. Yet the gospels record that Joseph was then spoken to in a dream revealing to him that what Mary had told him was true.

This wasn't just any birth. It was a Virgin Birth and a most miraculous birth. How sad that many churches in our world today do not believe what the Bible says about this miraculous birth. According to a poll in Red Book magazine 56% of newly ordained ministers do not believe in the virgin birth, yet if Jesus had a human father then He was just a sinful man who would also need a saviour. Christ, however, did not have a human/biological father. Instead the Spirit of God performed the paternal act in Mary's womb. Imagine the reaction to the news of her pregnancy. Public opinion would have been against Mary. That's why the Bible presents many witnesses to confirm that the virgin birth really happened and was a gift to our world from Almighty God. In fact, centuries prior to the birth of Christ, Isaiah one of the Bible's greatest ever prophets, wrote "Therefore the Lord Himself shall give you a sign; Behold a virgin shall conceive and bear a son and shall call his name Immanuel (God with us)", (Isaiah 7:14). Further evidence appeared in the New Testament from Elizabeth, Mary's cousin, (Luke 1:40-44), from Mary herself (Luke 1:34), from the angel Gabriel (Luke 1:35), from Joseph (Matthew 1:20), from Paul the apostle (Galatians 4:4) and finally from Almighty God Himself (Matthew 3:17).

Of course, over the years many have heard the story of the birth of Christ and what it signified, but have failed to grasp the immensity of it. Despite the countless onlookers who would have queued up for a peek at the miraculous newborn, the Bible records that only the three wise men came into the room where He was born. "And going into the house, they saw the child with Mary his mother and they fell down and worshipped Him" (Matthew 2:11). These wise men knew in their hearts that this was no ordinary baby lying before them. In that humble little stable lay a King with the greatest calling ever undertaken—to save the souls of mankind. This small, insignificant little town of Bethlehem and its inhabitants had been singled out as the place where the King of glory would be born. They were chosen of God to receive the greatest gift the world had ever known. "And thou Bethlehem, in the land of Juda, art not the least among the princes of Judah, for out of thee shall come a Governor, that shall rule my people Israel" (Matthew 2:6).

The wise men had followed Him there due to many earlier prophecies that He would indeed become great. Clearly they discerned that Jesus Christ, while still a baby, would grow up not just a King but was indeed the King of Kings and the Lord of all Lords. He more than anyone in history had the capacity to transform lives in ways not previously imagined. Instead of announcing the birth of this King to the prominent politicians and citizens of the land, however, the angels proclaimed it to lowly shepherds and three wise men all of whom were duly selected to be present at the most miraculous and blessed birth in history. Imagine what it must have been like for the wise men to witness this great birth? They had followed the star from the east eventually leading them to the very cradle of the Son of

God. What must they have thought once they finally established in their hearts that lying before them was the promised Messiah? Great prophets had come and gone and yet none of these had the privilege of seeing the Christ of God. Andrew the disciple once told his brother Peter after his own encounter with Jesus: "We have found the Messiah, which is, being interpreted, the Christ" (John 1:41). So, too, these wise men got a glimpse of glory that day and even visualised the joy and immense love that this baby would bring into the world.

The book of James states "Every good and perfect gift is from above, and comes down from the Father of lights with whom there is no variableness nor shadow of turning" (James 1:17). Problem is, many times we not only fail to recognise God's gifts in our lives, we also take them for granted. In the days of Christ, seasons of great joy were often accompanied by the giving of gifts, one to another. Today we call this season "Christmas time" when the joyful tidings of the angels reverberate in millions of family circles around the world. However, God's gift to mankind, Jesus Christ, is to be appreciated and shared daily with others. Human gifts are inconsistent, but good and perfect gifts are constant and come only from above, from the Father of lights. Giving began with God when He shared the gift of creation with men. Think of how God gave what we know as the universe itself to men and it was good and perfect. Voltaire once said "God gave us the gift of life; it's up to us to give ourselves the gift of living well".

Are we thankful for the blessings of God in our lives such as food, drink, a roof over our heads and a form of employment? In Romania many of these things were not freely available, yet in other parts of the world sadly they are taken for granted.

As I began to minister in Romania, it immediately struck me how selfish and ungrateful of God's gifts I had been for most of my own life. How I had taken for granted the basic, yet necessary every day blessings God regularly bestowed upon me. Blessings such as food, water, light and heat, peace in my heart, air to breathe and God's magnificent creation to observe each and every day free of charge. Jesus wanted us to recognise that God gives us wonderful gifts stating "If ye then being evil, know how to give good gifts unto your children, how much more shall your Father which is in heaven, give good things to them that ask him" (Matthew 7:11).

Solomon wrote "Every man also to whom God has given riches and wealth and hath given him power to eat thereof and to take his portion and to rejoice in his labour, this is the gift of God". (Ecclesiastes 5:19).

When God sent Jesus Christ His Son into the world He gave us His greatest gift of all, a gift not truly appreciated by His creation. When Jesus spoke to the woman at the well, He remarked to her "If thou knew the gift of God thou would have asked of him" (John 4:10). In other words, Christ told her "contained within me are all the gifts anyone can require"—the gift of the Holy Spirit, the gift of eternal life, the gift of individual personal abilities, the gift of salvation through faith and the gift of love, to name only a few.

This baby grew to spread the gospel of love, joy and peace throughout the earth. He matured and became the very Saviour of the world. His presence would be an assurance like no other for when Christ enters our hearts He transforms our future and the peace of God that passes all understanding is constantly at work in our lives. When we truly understand that He is the greatest of all gifts, we can only respond in praise and in wonder. We begin to understand the words of Paul the apostle "Thanks be unto God for His unspeakable gift" (2 Corinthians 9:15). That unspeakable gift is Jesus Christ; He's God's great gift to the world.

CHAPTER TWO

A DOG IS FOR LIFE, NOT JUST FOR CHRISTMAS

"And there was no room for him at the inn" (Luke 2:7)

LESSON 2—PREJUDICE POISONS THE TRUTH

The first Saturday Snowbell arrived at our house turned out to be most strange. Normally the children would all be back safely by four in the afternoon, but it was well past five and there was no sign of them. Suddenly I heard the gate opening allowing the bus to pull into the driveway. The kids sounded unusually hysterical, but in a very happy sense. As they rushed into the house, I could hear shouts of "Pastor John, Pastor John, Mama has something to show you". "I'm busy", I replied. "I'll be down in a minute". "Oh please, please, come quickly, Pastor John", some of the children insisted. "You have to see this", they continued eagerly

As usual I gave in, mainly because I was so curious about what it was that Mama had actually brought home. I glanced through my office window to observe what all the commotion was about and there was Mama completely surrounded by the children. Although I noticed something fluffy in her hands I also hoped it wasn't what I had imagined it to be. I walked down our three-tier staircase, almost nervously. It was as if I could sense the shock that lay in store for me. I had a gut feeling that this wasn't going to be one of those nice surprises in life

As I opened the kitchen door and emerged into our purpose-built park, which lay adjacent to the house, I detected the excitement of the children, some of whom just couldn't contain the secret any longer. "Mama bought us a dog", announced one of the younger girls. Our kids just had a knack of telling you things straight. "You are joking, aren't you", I retorted. "No, look here, Pastor John, his name is Snowbell, isn't he beautiful?" I tried to look pleased for them, but inside I was livid. Grinning through my teeth I asked, "Why Snowbell?" They went on to tell me it was because their newly acquired little white puppy resembled the white cat in the children's movie Stuart Little Two, one of their favourites at that time. "Ah right, that's clever," I responded. "So where's he going to stay then?" I asked; an obvious question, or so I thought! "In the bedroom next door to us," said Mama, as if that was in some way normal for two people who had never owned a dog before. "No way," I immediately protested, "I don't want that dog within a million miles of our apartment".

It was then that my true feelings were horribly revealed. All those years of dog-bites and dog-prejudice suddenly came to the fore. "I hate dogs, and I don't want one here", I blurted out. At that very moment several of the younger ones turned on the waterworks and I knew I had a serious problem. Looking back, it probably wasn't the greatest line I'd ever uttered. "Alright, he can stay, providing he doesn't come into the house", I said with authority, even though the kids and Mama were calling all the shots. The statement worked. The waterworks instantly decreased, much to my relief. "Where will the dog sleep, Pastor John?" asked Mama and the children. "That's your problem. You purchased him and you brought him, so you find somewhere for him to live", came my cold response. I went back upstairs to work on my sermon for the following day at church, yet no sooner had I begun writing again when another interruption occurred. "Pastor John, Mama has found Snowbell a house" echoed the sound of another little voice travelling all the way up the stairs. "That's great, who has agreed to take him off our hands", I countered optimistically. "Just come and see", insisted the child.

Once again I left my work and started the long walk to the bottom floor. I was like a man going for a hanging. Every step was slow, painful and thoughtful. I knew they had all found a way of keeping this dog within the grounds of our home, regardless of my best protests not to own any dog. I just didn't know where its location would be. When I emerged into the garden, I was taken to a little alley-way between the children's classroom and the church we had built beside the home. It was well covered over and actually looked like an old air-raid shelter. When I looked inside, there he was; the new puppy, wrapped in a blanket and sitting in a little basket surrounded by onlookers. Even strangers from the street had converged on our home for a look at our new family pet. I immediately felt quite guilty. After all, we had made room for many homeless and unwanted Romanian children within our home, so why couldn't I at least have compassion for this little Romanian puppy? The thought occurred to me how he had been shut outside the house all because of me and the hardness of my heart. I felt safer condemning this dog to the make-shift dog kennel, than to let him inside our home. I didn't feel great about it, but it was my decision and I was sticking to it.

The book of Luke records that when Jesus was a baby He too was shut outside of the house, due to the hardness of many hearts. Luke chapter 2 and verse 7 describes how His mother Mary brought forth her first-born son, and wrapped Him in swaddling clothes and laid Him in a manger. The Bible says that there just wasn't any room for Him at the inn.

The people of Christ's day had been told that the Saviour of the world would be born in Bethlehem in the days of Herod the King. It would prove a humble start for someone who would grow up to be crowned King of Kings. Could this King possibly be born in a stable and then found wrapped in swaddling clothes and lying in a manger? For thousands of years the Israelites expected their Messiah to come in kingly fashion, but instead God chose a manger, the humblest dwelling. The King of the Jews they expected would surely be hailed as front page news; require trumpets, a large stage, a feast, fireworks and probably a guard of honour, too. Surely no king would turn up in the shape of a tiny new-born in a stall surrounded by animals and straw? Could this king be born without a proper roof over his head? Is it further possible that no room could be found for such a baby, especially if the future predicted for Him was so great? It was not only possible, it happened and, in many ways, it's been happening ever since. Even today many people simply have no room in their hearts for Jesus. In the same way that I had no regard for Snowbell and confined him to the outside yard, men and women of all persuasions and nations regularly refuse to open their hearts to the love of Christ. We're too busy, too arrogant, too religious, too cold, too full of prejudice, too fearful and even too stubborn. We allow many trivial things to dominate our lives, yet we have no room for the King of Glory. Even on Christmas Day, millions prefer presents to worship. They eat turkey, drink wine and make merry, but there's no room for Jesus. Knowledge and technology may have increased, but mankind appears just as selfish as the day Christ was born well over 2000 years ago. People are not necessarily opposed to God; they are just preoccupied; thus God and spiritual things are put on the backburner. Could this be what happened in the case of the innkeeper? Perhaps he was just too busy to make room for the soon-coming Messiah.

All messianic prophecies relating to the birth of Christ from the Hebrew prophets clearly highlight the book of Isaiah and chapter nine where it is written "Unto us a child is born, unto us a son is given and the government shall be upon his shoulder, he shall be called Wonderful, Counsellor, Mighty God, Everlasting Father, Prince of Peace" (Isaiah 9:6-7).

The gospels also emphasize how the child was born in Bethlehem, the town of Joseph's origin. As Bethlehem brimmed with returning peasants due to the Roman census, the family were forced to stay in a barn. Think about it! In the providence of God, the world's Messiah was born beside the animals. He was born in what the Bible describes as "a manger". This should astound mankind. Jesus Christ, the King of Kings and Lord of Lord's wasn't born in a prosperous, snug home. He was born in a stable where animals were kept. The question is, why? Even though by nature the Bible says that Jesus is God, it also records how this God chose not just a low place, but the lowest place for the birth of His Son. His desire was to "preach good news to the poor" so He was born among the poorest of the poor. Romania was full of poor people, but Christ was there every day. Lots of them lived in small village homes and most of them had animals, but they were not void of God's presence. Many would comment to me how God was "just a prayer away" and He was. They depended on God's goodness every day. We live in a world where so-called prosperity preachers show Christ allegedly circulating among the "rich" and, while He died and rose again for rich people, too, the plain fact is the Bible portrays Christ as one who circulated more among the poor for the common people heard him gladly. While His disciples argued about who would be greatest in the Kingdom, Jesus showed by example how to take the lowly position and serve. He told them "For the Son of Man did not come to be served, but to serve and to give his life a ransom for many" (Mark :10:45). The story of the birth of Christ teaches us humility and servanthood. It brings reality again to our lives. Has this story become so familiar to us that we have now completely missed the reason for the season? After all, the story is old and has been told well many, many times, the story of an inn, a pregnant virgin, a stable, a manger, a star and a king. Is it still possible for this generation to see this narrative in a fresh light and make room again for God's Son, even if our lives are packed with activities, toys and gadgets?

They say, "A dog is for life, not just for Christmas". This slogan was created in 1978 by Clarissa Baldwin, Chief Executive of the Dogs Trust and is just as relevant today. The long-standing campaign to raise awareness of the consequences of treating dogs as gifts or toys continues unabated. Yet every year hundreds of thousands of children plead for the latest fad or top toy on the market, only to discard them a few weeks after Christmas when the novelty wears off. Unfortunately, the same perception is also apparent with dogs, many of which are purchased for Christmas and then tossed aside like pieces of rubbish. It was concerning to observe just how many stray dogs were running wild in Romania. Many of them were killed on the roads because their owner had probably chosen to abandon them. Likewise, Jesus too is for life, yet many people bring Him out like a toy at Christmas, only to discard Him once the festive season is over. They attend church and become religious for one day and then abandon God, assuming He will be impressed with their one-off meagre sacrifice. Some only go to church on Christmas Eve in order to spend all day on themselves on Christmas Day. They don't want any guilt on their big day so they "do God a favour" as it were.

Are we any different from the days when Jesus walked the earth? The Bible says "He came unto his own, but his own received him not, but to as many as received him to them gave he power to become the sons of God, even to them that believe on his name". (John 1:11-12). In other words He came into the world that He had created only to be rejected and unrecognised. Despite performing many miracles, fulfilling predictions made of the coming Messiah, healing the sick, raising the dead and claiming to be God, many still chose to reject Him. Even some of His closest followers left Him and at His miraculous birth they couldn't even find a room for Him. What makes people reject Christ in this way? It is the very same thing that made me reject all dogs, even Snowbell initially. It's summed up in one word, prejudice. Even though I had never owned a dog, my view of these creatures was that they were smelly, needed fed too often, needed walked, barked too much, left their mess in the house and attacked people they didn't like, especially athletes! I had heard numerous negative stories about dogs and for whatever reason I just assumed they were all true.

The word prejudice simply means "to form an unfavourable opinion or feeling beforehand without thought, knowledge or reason". To assume that someone has an unusual unflattering set of characteristics just because they are part of some group, such as a particular race or religion is the worst kind of prejudice and, let's face it, such prejudice is alive and well in the world we live in today. People are not just prejudicial towards animals; they are becoming more and more intolerant of one another. There are numerous stabbings and muggings every week in the cities of our world due to the colour of someone's skin or due to their religious convictions. Even at key sports fixtures, racist abuse is still a major issue, both on and off the pitch and, despite the horrendous suffering incurred by the Jews during the horrific event known as "the Holocaust", there are those who continue to hold an anti-Semitic viewpoint even to the extent of violence.

The Bible says that Jesus was also a victim of violence and prejudice and was hated by the scribes and Pharisees. Isaiah records that "He was despised and rejected of men, a man of sorrows and acquainted with grief, and we hid as it were our faces from Him, he was despised and we esteemed him not" (Isaiah 53:3). Even in His home town of Nazareth, where he had no liberty to perform miracles due to their unbelief and great prejudice, Jesus was viewed as just the son of a carpenter and certainly not the Son of God. God is against prejudice and racism of any form. To estrange people from our church or home based upon the colour of their skin or ethnic background is most displeasing to God. In Romania many children were rejected and isolated solely because of the colour of their skin or social status. We would often have to come to the aid of children because they were unwanted elsewhere. This kind of rejection can be devastating to a person no matter what age they are and is not how God intended His creation to behave. It's been said that there's only one race—the human race. Caucasians, Africans, Asians, Indians, Arabs and Jews are not different races; they are different ethnicities of the human race. The book of Genesis tells us that all human beings are created in the image and likeness of God. (Genesis 1:26-27) while Paul writes "there is neither Jew nor Greek, slave nor free, male nor female, for you are all one in Christ Jesus. The Bible further tells us "For God so loved the world that he gave his only begotten son that whosoever believeth in him shall not perish but have everlasting life" (John 3:16). Clearly therefore God does not show partiality or favouritism and neither should we. Christ came to put an end to prejudice and elitism of this sort. As Paul writes, "For he himself is our peace, who has made us both one and broken down in his flesh the dividing wall of hostility" (Ephesians 2:14). All forms of racism, prejudice and discrimination are affronts to the work of Christ and the cross. Instead Christ commands us to love one another with impartiality. Racism, in varying forms and to various degrees has been a plague on humanity for thousands of years and prejudice has hindered many from coming to know and cherish the love of God. Many have rejected Christ purely on the basis of what someone else has said, while others have lost out in their spiritual walk because someone poisoned the denomination or church they were thinking of attending.

When we arrived in Romania many judged us based on things they had heard and not on what was actually fact. For years I did exactly the same thing with dogs. For example, had I known the love and blessing that Snowbell would ultimately bring to my life. I would most certainly have let him into the house to stay the very first day he arrived. What this dog would eventually add to my life was, and still is, beyond description. He would teach me that while not every person knows how to love a dog, every dog knows how to love a person. The fact that I lived many years without this love would ultimately prove to be of great regret to me.

I have found the same with many people who wait almost a lifetime before accepting Christ as their Saviour and then end up declaring, "If only I had known what a lovely Lord He would become, if only I had known what He would add to my life, I would have accepted Him gladly years ago".

Don't confine Him to some makeshift room outside the door of your heart. Don't judge Him because of what you have heard or what you have been taught. Instead, why not appreciate today what God did when He sent Jesus into the world? He offers you forgiveness, friendship and a future. If you let Him into your heart, He will surely take over and become the centre of attention in due course. If you finally make room for Him, He, more than anyone, has the power to change your thinking and your life forever. Remember, prejudice only poisons the truth.

CHAPTER THREE

INCREDIBLE GROWTH

("And the child grew, waxed strong in spirit, filled with
wisdom and the grace of God was upon Him").

LESSON 3—GROWTH IS NOT GROWTH WITHOUT GRACE AND TRUTH.

The sight of the tiny puppy cuddled up in his little basket brought absolutely no indication of the speed at which Snowbell would develop, nor of the strong dog he'd ultimately become. Within no time he had sprouted up and was sprinting around everywhere. Labradors are powerful, agile and full of energy when running about, which is why they are clearly not suited to apartment life or even to life in a house with a small garden. In this respect Snowbell was in his element as our Romanian home provided massive private grounds for him to take his daily exercise.

So rapid was his growth we even had to protect some of the smaller children as he rushed through the yard like a cyclone, knocking over anything in his path. Even the cute little basket he used to lie in had become far too small for his fast development. His puppy-like innocence brought no indication either of the tremendous intelligence he would later display, or even of the wonderful nature and love this dog was capable of bestowing. It was a balance that was actually quite remarkable. On the one hand he was strong and spirited, a really powerful dog. Yet on the other hand, here was an animal full of love and so incredibly smart and skilled, especially when it came to retrieving things of interest to him.

I recall watching him from my bedroom window as he paraded about the courtyard adjacent to our house. He was like a lion in the jungle. He would amble about seemingly not interested in anything, but such behaviour was merely pretence. This switched-on growing Labrador knew exactly what he was doing. Sizing up his prey, which would often be some poor little bird at the top of the garden, I could see him setting his sights before taking off like an Olympic sprinter to catch his victim and bring it back to anyone who was prepared to pat him on the back and say "well done". "Back from scattering birds, all dogs swagger a bit", wrote Dan Liebert and Snowbell was no exception. He always had a lofty opinion of himself.

Snowbell clearly displayed great wisdom, even guile, as he went about his business, something which was fascinating to watch. By contrast was the exceptional manner in which he also grew to be a particularly loving and beautiful dog, which he seemed blatantly aware of. Renowned as the best family dog to own, Snowbell knew he was a top breed. He would often look at poodles and other dogs as though they were members of some weird religious cult. He was so beautiful he could stop traffic—a long-eared George Clooney. People often remarked on his posture and on his adorable features. "What a beautiful looking dog you have", they would comment. Then, as if he understood exactly what they were saying, Snowbell would offer them his paw and another friend and admirer was secured. He became not just man's best friend, but my best friend and even helped me find friendship in others. I would regularly sit outside the house beside him and before I knew it, numerous people would stop and ask "Your dog is so cute! Would you mind if I stroked him?" He was simply irresistible and only now, of course, do I realise what dog enthusiasts are sometimes so gaga about.

It was a similar story with the children at our home, especially the younger girls. They were always turned out so beautifully in their little dresses and shoes. All of them had to have their hair styled "personally" by Mama Louise and their appearance caught the attention of people everywhere when we took them into the city. One day after arriving at McDonald's the staff stopped taking other customers just to fit us all in and the people were fascinated as they peered through the glass at all of the little girls in their dresses and shoes. Even the little boys in their Sunday suits looked so cute, yet it wouldn't be long before all of them had outgrown those same clothes and developed and matured before our very eyes. We constantly had to invest in new shoes, new coats and practically new "everything" on behalf of the children, many of whom seemed to spring up almost unnoticed. It was still beautiful to watch the excitement in the little girls as they fixed their hair and put on make-up for the first time, not to mention how the boys looked so macho in new jeans, trainers and a cool t-shirt. Their voices and mannerisms had changed, too, and you could just see them growing into beautiful young men and women. Jesus Himself matured quickly to reveal his own amazing qualities, unforeseen by various men and women of His own generation, and in no time revealed how Christian growth is imperative in the lives of Christians. The book of Luke says of Christ's own development: "And the child grew, waxed strong in spirit, filled with wisdom and the grace of God was upon Him" (Luke 2:40). It's often easily forgotten how Jesus Christ is not only the Son of God; He also became the Son of Man on our behalf. The title "Son of Man" is a reference to His great humanity and nowhere is this more evident than with the statement "And the child grew".

Try and grasp how God sent His only Son from glory to live a life just like us! Consider this! The Prince of Glory, the creator of the universe and everything in it, became a little child and took on a human body. Conceived of the Holy Ghost and sinless in every way, He sat where we sit and lived as we live. The Son of God, who was perfect in every way, descended to earth in human form in order to identify with every part of our own humanity. The writer of the book of Hebrews says: "For we have not a high priest which cannot be touched by the feelings of our infirmities, but was in all points tempted like as we are, yet without sin" (Hebrews 4:15

Think about it, He grew just like any other baby. His mother Mary would have had to feed Him, dress Him, teach Him to walk and to talk; nevertheless He grew quickly and impressively. We know this because of the story in Luke chapter 2 when, as a twelve-year-old boy, Jesus confounded the religious leaders of that day by hearing them and asking them remarkable questions. Luke records that, despite being so young, they were astonished both at His understanding and at the answers which He gave. His parents,

Mary and Joseph, had lost Him three days earlier and were searching for Him. However when they found the boy and asked where He had been, Jesus simply answered "How is it that you sought me, did you not know that I must be about my Father's business" (Luke 2:49). From a young age, Christ was always interested and involved in the business of His Father. During Christ's earthly life His fortitude and strength was also there for all to see. We read of how He matured and grew in strength to the extent that He took on those same scribes and Pharisees He had impressed many years before, after it was discovered they were involved in extortion within the house of God. Overturning the tables of the money changers, Jesus told them: "It is written, my house shall be called a house of prayer, but you have turned it into a den of thieves" (Matthew 21:13). We read also how He stood up to Pilate and to the authorities before His death on the cross; how He even endured the excruciating pain of that same cross for our sins. What strength and courage He demonstrated!

Many times the wisdom of Christ was evident too. Surrounded by people just waiting to trip Him up, notwithstanding He knew how to answer His critics. One particular incident is a case in point. A woman caught in the act of adultery had the crowd baying for her blood. Casually Jesus stooped down and wrote on the ground, buying time for himself, before silencing them with the statement: "He that is without sin among you, let him cast the first stone". No-one dared! Much wisdom and grace was required in Romania. Spiritual growth would be necessary or else we would undoubtedly struggle to adapt to a culture we had absolutely no experience of. Observing Snowbell's own growth from a puppy into a powerful strong dog reminded me, too, of just how much growth is required in the Christian life before we reach this place of strength and grace. We do not become the finished product overnight. There's a process of growth to be experienced and, in some cases, endured.

Peter the apostle exhorts us to "grow in grace and in the knowledge of our Lord and Saviour Jesus Christ" (2 Peter 3:18). Christian growth has rightly been described as "progressive sanctification". As we grow in grace, we are gradually changing to be more like Jesus due to a process of daily spiritual renewal. As Paul writes "And have put on the new man, who is renewed in knowledge after the image of him that created him" (Colossians 10:3). This is simply referred to as "the new birth". Just as we were delighted to see the children growing and maturing before our very eyes, did you know that God is blessed when He sees His own children maturing in a spiritual sense? God desires for us to move from the spiritual nursery, if you like, to the spiritual battlefield. He wants us to grow and reach spiritual maturity. There are too many "cry-babies" in the church; men and women who, in a spiritual context, have never left childhood. These are people who have never developed and who regularly rebel when they don't get everything their own way. But Christians need to grow up in God if they are to influence the world in which we live.

Just as children desire to grow to be like their parents, the child of God should desire to grow more like Jesus. They are constantly adapting their lives to the teachings of the Bible. John writes "Now by this we know that we know Him, if we keep His commandments, he who says I know Him and does not keep His commandments is a liar, and the truth is not in him" (1 John 2:-4). Christian growth is evident when we enjoy devotional times with God, have a personal relationship with Jesus and a personal walk with God. The Christian has learned to shun the pleasures of this world and has separated from the works of darkness. There's a fresh need to walk in the path the Lord has laid out. Life ceases to be about "self will" and instead becomes more about God's will. That's why the Bible identifies the believer as "a new creature" (2 Corinthians 5:7). When all of us start out in the Christian life we are still quite self-centred, but as we grow in God, this selfish existence begins to disappear and suddenly we recognise more the needs of others. Growing in God is growing in love for others. Jesus said as much with the words "A new commandment I give unto you that you love one another" (John 13:35). Hindrances to Christian growth and maturity, however, are far too common. The Bible warns us "Be sober, be vigilant, for your adversary (the devil) as a roaring lion, walks about, seeking whom he may devour" (1 Peter 5:8). They had a saying in Romania, namely, "How do you spoil a man's dream?" Answer "Give him another one". The devil is a master at giving us another idea. Many times I would be tempted to digress from my assignment after being approached by others with another idea. Stick to the plan. Stay focused on the original task God gave you to do. Anything else can hinder growth and foil the purpose of God in your life. Paul wrote "Ye did run well, who did hinder you that you should not obey the truth" (Galatians 5:7). One translation of this verse reads: "You were running the race well, what caused you to stumble". The world and our flesh is our greatest adversary. The devil and the world work together to stunt Christian growth and no more so than in the revealing and acknowledging of God's grace in our lives. While we were relatively experienced Christians during our time in Romania, it's fair to say that in terms of ministry and missionary work we were still babies and God would teach us many lessons, not least that no matter what kind of spiritual warfare we may have been facing, gentleness is a fruit of the spirit and the main reason we had come to Romania was to help people. The goal of every believer is to help, comfort and restore. This is the very nature of God. It was very tempting to become embroiled in arguments in Romania, especially with the authorities, who seemed to perpetually bother our home about trivial matters. But conflict distracts us from our goals and dreams. Wisdom and gentleness is required in order to remain focused and to keep growing in God. James writes "But the wisdom that is from above is first pure, then peaceable and gentle, and easy to be entreated, full of mercy and good fruits, without partiality and without hypocrisy (James 3:17). As God showed us these things, we soon learned that to win the convert a large amount of grace is necessary.

Jesus told His followers to be "wise as serpents and harmless as doves" (Matthew 10:16). Certainly Christ's most beautiful attribute was the amazing grace He displayed during His life and the love that He offered to lost sinners and still offers today due to His sinless life, sacrificial death and wonderful resurrection. The proof of a Christ-like man or woman is one who is both strong and kind at the same time. This is evident Christian growth. Standing up for Jesus is not a sign of Christian growth, becoming like Him is the real proof. Many preachers tell their congregations to stand up for Jesus, yet they themselves are nothing like Him. How demoralising is this? Sadly, while full of zeal and good intentions, these erroneous evangelists present a wrong and misleading interpretation of the gospel to our lost and despairing generation. It's not just important to present the gospel; presenting the gospel in the right way and in God's way is also fundamental. To "rightly divide the word of truth" as Paul the apostle puts it, is of equal importance and, rightly dividing the word of truth, is explaining the gospel as Christ explained it. In His earthly life, Christ grew to display great power, strength and wisdom and even used anger at selective and appropriate times, yet He was bursting with incredible grace. His purpose is not that any should perish, but rather that men and women might be saved through His immense love and sacrifice at Calvary. This, I believe, is what Peter was primarily referring to when he used the phrase "Grow in grace and in the knowledge of our Lord and Saviour Jesus Christ". While Christ has ultimate authority, and is full of truth, He is also brimming with grace and unconditional love, making Him a most balanced God. You may conquer the world, you may build a great ministry, but without grace and truth working side by side you will most likely leave a trail of destruction behind you. How precious are the words of Jesus—"For God sent not his Son into the world to condemn the world, but that the world through him might be saved" (John 3:17). The book of John also refers to Him as a man "Full of grace and truth" (John 1:14). John goes on to say that such grace and truth came to our world by one way and one way alone—Jesus Christ Himself.

Just as Snowbell gently used to offer his paw to people passing by, every day the Saviour of the world offers the gift of salvation to a needy and broken planet. He doesn't shout, force, or intimidate, he doesn't use fear tactics or bribery; instead He quietly and softly calls wayward men and women unto Himself. His mission is not to condemn, but to restore. From the time of His miraculous birth until His sacrificial death on the cross at Calvary, Christ's growth was incredible, especially in the revealing of His boundless love—a love that, even today, makes Him irresistible and such a beautiful Lord!

CHAPTER FOUR

———————

DON'T BE SO JEALOUS!

"You shall not bow down to them or worship them, for I the
Lord your God am a jealous God" (Exodus 20:5).

LESSON 4—NOT ALL JEALOUSY IS BAD!

Following the birth of any baby, it's not long before the trait of
jealousy appears. Children, of course, can quickly become jealous
of siblings and anything that may detract attention away from
them. Notwithstanding, it's still a shock to witness those first indications
of jealousy in any child, and equally so when jealousy relates to a dog.
Having read about the behavioural traits of the Labrador, I now know that
the golden retriever puppy is a wonderfully playful pet, with a placid and
very friendly personality, yet I am reliably informed by the dog experts of
this world that these animals also have a genuine tendency toward jealousy.

The first time I saw Snowbell show jealousy, I actually burst out laughing,
but I must confess it also left me feeling quite shocked. Having had no
previous experience of a dog's personality, I assumed jealousy was something
only we humans are capable of displaying. I had heard of the jealousy of
Saul in the Bible prior to David becoming King and the jealousy of a lover
not happy with the attention being shown to his or her "prize possession".
I had even witnessed the jealousy of some of the children at our home: but
the jealousy of a dog? That was something altogether new to me.

He was still a pup when this notable side of his character first emerged. When I would hug, kiss and show affection to someone other than Snowbell, he would begin barking loudly and even became aggressive at times, which wasn't at all like him. The first time this "dog-demon" so to speak was unleashed proved a real eye-opener for both me and my wife. It was evening play time in a spare room we had created for Snowbell where all of his toys were assembled. There was a cupboard full of dog food and other goodies and two large beds which he loved to jump on before lying down and getting his evening massage; a hard life, but someone had to do it! Then one evening Louise took one of his toys, a little doll with long straggly hair. Softly she began to caress the doll in the same way she would normally stroke Snowbell. "There's a good girl," said Louise as she gently patted the little doll's back. What happened next is still imprinted upon my memory many years later. Our dog literally jumped up into the air and snatched the doll out of Louise's hand and raced off down the stairs. We wondered what had just taken place. It was so unlike him, yet it was obvious that he wasn't best pleased at Louise's decision to give attention to someone other than him. We could smell jealousy in the air, but we could hardly believe it. When we rushed to investigate where he'd gone, we found the doll lying round the back of the house with its head almost torn off. Snowbell had just given us the most graphic picture of his jealous nature. At first I assumed he was jealous because we had taken his toy, but that wasn't it at all. We used to lift other toys and he never reacted in such a violent manner. No, the reason Snowbell not only wrested the toy from Louise's possession and ran outside and practically destroyed it, was simply because he couldn't bear to watch us giving our love to someone other than him. We know this because following this incident similar behaviour would flare up from time to time when anyone else was given special praise in his company. Simply put, he was a jealous little dog at times

They say "jealousy is as cruel as the grave" and certainly most forms of jealousy are indeed quite controlling and ultimately destructive. When the women of David's generation in the Old Testament came out to applaud him they made a fatal mistake by declaring that Saul, who was King, had slain his thousands but David his ten thousands" (I Samuel 1 18:7). This admiration and show of affection in favour of David angered Saul so much that the Bible records "from that day forward Saul eyed David". In other words, Saul marked David, singled him out as a man to watch. He made him a rival instead of a friend and thus displayed the trait of jealousy that has ruined lesser men than Saul. Our reaction reveals our character and, if we are not careful, the consequences can be grave.

The book of Esther records a powerful tale of jealousy that not only rebounded on an individual called Haman; it also had a dreadful after-effect on his ten sons. Haman was a descendent of Agag, the king of the Amalekites, a people who were wiped out in certain areas by King Saul and King David. For revenge, Haman and his wife plotted to kill all Jews of ancient Persia and one of the driving factors in this decision was Haman's great jealousy of a Jew named Mordechia. Haman erected gallows for Mordechia, but was hung on them himself along with his ten sons after the plot to kill Mordechia and the Jews failed.

Joseph was his dad's favourite son. He had big dreams and aspirations in life. After his father made him a special coat, Joseph's brothers became incredibly jealous of him. Soon they began to hate him and eventually threw him into a pit and sold him into slavery in Egypt. To most of us, jealousy has a negative connotation. We know that it can lead to such things as covetousness, bitterness, envy and hatred. In the story of Cain, his jealousy grew until he rose up and murdered his brother Abel. When Daniel was promoted to Prime Minister, the rest of the princes became so jealous of him they sought to destroy him with a wicked plan. Jealous feelings start with something as small as not liking someone, but if we allow them to grow, we can become filled with hatred. Are you jealous of a brother or sister who gets more attention than you or someone is chosen for a job or position you thought was yours? The result of jealousy can be quite catastrophic. Read the news headlines these days and commonplace are stories about men and women who have taken the lives of their spouses or partners after flying into a jealous rage. Some of those victims had been knifed or shot to death, following a violent outburst from their so-called lover. Others decide to premeditate the murder by plotting in advance how to dispose of their partner, such was their inability to control their jealousy. Jealousy of this kind is indeed a most poisonous thing and should never be made light of.

Solomon, in the book of Proverbs, wrote "Wrath is cruel, anger is overwhelming, but who can stand before jealousy?" (Proverbs 27:4).

Galatians chapter five and verse twenty describes this kind of jealousy as a sin. The word jealous is an unattractive word. "It is the green-eyed monster", said Shakespeare in Othello. It has overtones of selfishness, suspicion and distrust and implies a shocking resentment or hostility to other people who seem to be doing better in life. It is controlling, self-centred and overbearing and that is abhorrent. It blocks freedom and distinctiveness, it degrades and demeans, it breeds anxiety and dissension, it destroys friendships and marriages. Jealousy is viewed as a horrible attribute. Jealousy believes another received what you deserved and sadly this jealousy also exists within the church and by the people of God, something which was proven by the dreadful reaction of Joseph's brothers. How far removed all of this is from the writings of Paul who states "be kindly affectionate one to another with brotherly love; in honour preferring one another" (Romans 12:10).

I am convinced that the root cause of many of our problems in Romania was not a misunderstanding of religions, or necessarily a struggle of who was right or wrong; instead I believe the underlying factor in us receiving frequent persecution was the sin of jealousy. People were jealous of the quality of our home, they were jealous of our staff and of the style and privileges our children inherited. Some were even jealous of Louise and I because we had been chosen by God to fulfil His task. This jealousy is often hidden and doesn't stop until it destroys. It can become a major enemy to a Christian and is just as prevalent within one's own family, church or community. Remember the Bible says "A man's enemies shall be of his own house".

It's sad to think that people within our own family or our own church would actually attempt to conspire against us in order to see us fail. Yet this has been the case for centuries and the usual cause of this form of betrayal is the sin of jealousy. However, the point to make in Snowbell's defence is that he was probably displaying an altogether more acceptable form of jealousy, albeit his methods of dealing with it were certainly questionable at that stage. I remember saying to him "Don't be so jealous", but he looked at me with those big sad, loving eyes as if to say "you don't understand, it's because I love you that I behaved the way I did".

This made me instantly conscious of another kind of jealousy which isn't bad at all! We have all probably thought that there's no way God can be associated with jealousy! But is this so? In both the Old and New Testaments, the words for jealousy are also translated as "zeal". Being jealous and being zealous therefore is essentially the same thing in the Bible. In other words, God is zealous, eager about protecting what is precious to Him. In fact, this form of jealousy is pure and kind and even acceptable. While such jealousy is rarely evident in the nature of men, it clearly exists within the nature of God. Like Snowbell, my wonderful pet, God has a very jealous nature—a permissible and beautiful form of jealousy. This jealousy is not to destroy us, but to save us from devastation. It operates when the child of God commits spiritual adultery by following after strange and false gods.

When you and I show our affection for another god, the Father becomes jealous of us in a protective way. There's a powerful illustration of this found in the book of Exodus where God rebuked the children of Israel with the words "You shall not bow down to them or worship them, for I the Lord your God am a jealous God" (Exodus 20:5). In other words God is grieved when we turn our attention to other gods who cannot save us or redeem our lives One of God's names is the word—jealous. Isn't that amazing! Yet because He is full of goodness, it naturally follows there must be something positive and instructive about jealousy. A mind-blowing thought is: can God be jealous to the point of envy? Can He be jealous of someone or something? Can he be bitter and selfishly possessive? Like many other attributes of God, Satan has tried his best to distort our understanding of jealousy and to make us believe the negative. The dictionary's definition of the word jealous has two main meanings: "intolerance of rivalry or unfaithfulness" or "guarding a possession". Both these aspects apply to the nature of God. While He is forgiving and patient and even understanding, His heart is also grieved when we draw back from Him in favour of other gods or individuals. He wants to guard and protect us from that which is destructive and so His jealousy becomes a pure form of jealousy and a most beautiful demonstration of His great love for us. In its definition of jealousy, the American Heritage Dictionary reads "fearful or wary of being supplanted, apprehensive of losing affection or position.

Paul writes, "For I am jealous for you with godly jealousy. For I have betrothed you to one husband, that I may present you as a chaste virgin to Christ". What was the object of Paul's jealousy? Was it to have the people for him? No, he was closely guarding these same people with godly jealousy in order to present them virtuous to Christ. Paul was not jealous "of" these people, but "for" them. The Bible says God is a jealous God and a consuming fire. When God delivered the Ten Commandments to Moses in the book of Exodus saying, "I the Lord am a jealous God", He did so to highlight to the children of Israel that there were to be no other gods held before Him. God requires the number one spot in our lives. In other words God is intolerant of rivalry, wouldn't you say? He is intolerant of unfaithfulness. When Jesus made that powerful statement "I am the way, the truth and the life, no man comes to the Father but by Me" (John 14:6), He was not being bigoted or even arrogant, he was merely stating a fact in order to fully expose every false cult in the world.

Of course animals like Snowbell do not have a carnal human nature, but we can still learn from some of their actions. In the same way Snowbell wanted all of our affections for himself, so too God wants our love to be exclusively His. This form of jealousy is healthy and normal, but only if we can control our response to it which Snowbell obviously couldn't and many mere mortals have struggled with it also; yet not God. His response is always measured and controlled. He wants the best for us. He will never seek to control us or make us feel suffocated, but His love is still willing to fight for our affection at all times.

If we decide to wander or stray, that's when God becomes jealous for our wellbeing and even jealous for our love. St Augustine once wrote "he that is not jealous is not in love". How true of God's great love for us. God loves us so much He is concerned about every aspect of our lives and wants us to be blessed by this love only. It's the best example of fatherly love available. It's been said "the proof of love is the obsession to protect" and this is how God's great love manifests itself towards His children. It's a protective and pure form of love, but in return God requires our love for Him to be exclusive.

Remember what Jesus said at the Mount of Temptation—"get thee hence Satan for it is written, you shall worship the Lord your God and Him only shall you serve" (Matthew 4:10). Jehovah is the one true God and He wants no one else to get in the way! Isn't that a wonderful and committed love? Isn't that a refreshing form of jealousy? And, incidentally, who would dare to say to God, like I said to Snowbell my dog "Don't be so jealous!"

CHAPTER FIVE

BORN TO GRACE THE MOUNTAINS

"Whom the Son sets free is free indeed" (John 8:36)

LESSON 5—WE ARE BORN TO RUN.

One of the most heart-touching memories I recall about Snowbell in Romania was the look on his face when we had to leave him behind in his little hut. As the car pulled out of our driveway he would just sit and stare knowing he would be housebound for the next number of hours. It was as though he was being held captive, a prisoner in his own home. I'm convinced that "that stare" which he would always employ was no accident. It was a manipulative message sent to prick my conscience. How dare I leave him behind chained up in such a cruel way!

Snowbell always seemed to know, too, when we were about to go out, because we would watch him slinking off to begin his emotional blackmail scene. Don't think he didn't know what he was doing? I read recently how researchers in Japan have shown conclusively that dogs can even recognise a human smile. A team at Azabu University found that dogs were far more drawn to photographs of their owners in which those owners were smiling. Within a few seconds of departing the house, they are equally aware that we are getting ready to leave and encouraging others to "hurry up", and that's when they become anxious and their behavioural pattern changes.

Such manipulation by Snowbell almost worked on numerous occasions for my heart sank when I saw him sitting forlorn like that. I knew he hated being locked up for any length of time, but for his own safety and the safety of others we had to ensure he was securely stationed in his hut albeit for just a short period of time. I disliked seeing him fret like that just as much as he appeared to resent the fact that we actually had a life other than his. What a contrast when we would return to the house later the same evening, park the car and unlock the gate of Snowbell's hut! At that point the dog would literally sprint out and jump chest high to greet us. He would emerge from his little "afternoon prison cell" as it were with the most remarkable enthusiasm. He was so overwhelmingly grateful we had returned to set him free. As I would later find out when the true nature and purpose of this dog became more apparent to me, Snowbell's sad countenance when we left him and joyful spring in his step later when we returned were only symptomatic of his true character and triggered by his inner greatness—the need to be a champion dog. A Labrador isn't born to lie in the valley; he's literally born to grace the mountains.

Peter Neville, in his excellent book about the Labrador, describes how this dog was originally bred as a working dog and even today many Labradors are kept as gun dogs, guide dogs, service dogs and search and rescue dogs. This animal is incredibly flexible and useful. Labradors are frequently used to seek out prohibited drugs; they act as guide dogs and have become marvellous in helping the disabled. Peter Neville outlines how this breed has its origins in Newfoundland on the east coast of Canada. In the early 1800's fishermen from many parts of Europe travelled to the cod banks of Newfoundland, where there were two types of working dog. One type was more heavily built, large and with a longish coat, whereas the other was lighter in build, an active, smooth-coated water-dog. The larger, heavier dog was called the Newfoundland; but the lighter type, the St John's breed of Newfoundland, was called the Labrador retriever. The St. John's water dog, also known as the St. John's dog or the lesser Newfoundland, was the ancestor of the modern retrievers, including the Flat Coated Retriever, the Chesapeake Bay Retriever, the Golden Retriever and the Labrador Retriever

It's clear the Labrador retriever was born for a mountain-top experience. He wasn't meant to be chained up all day; on the contrary his energy levels demanded that he got out regularly working, running and playing.

This is also the plan and purpose of God for every Christian. We have been born slaves to Satan and to sin (2 Timothy 2:26). Like the children of Israel, under the rule of Egypt, we are strangers in an alien land; powerless it appears to remedy our situation until Christ comes and delivers us out of our darkness. Prior to our salvation experience with Christ we are all held captive and in chains by Satan. We are in various prisons of sin. These prisons are packed with drug addicts, alcoholics, and those addicted to many other life-ruining vices. The common denominator among all of them is the fact that not a single person is happy. Crestfallen faces are everywhere because deep down in every human being is an immense desire to grace the mountains just like the Labrador retriever.

The Bible compares the child of God to an eagle in the book of Isaiah. "They which wait on the Lord shall renew their strength, they shall mount up with wings as eagles, they shall run and not be weary, they shall walk and not faint" (Isaiah 40:31). It's hard to soar like an eagle when we are surrounded by a bunch of turkeys, which happens when we choose to live beneath God's standards for our lives, or allow circumstances to hold us back, but according to Isaiah, even in the worst of weather, we can all soar on eagles' wings. The eagle is the king of birds and is a symbol of strength. Even the Air Force has a plane called the Eagle F-15 that is unequalled in its ability as a fighter jet. An eagle flies to live and he lives to fly. Have you ever seen an eagle hobbling along the ground? An eagle is born to spread its wings and fly and this is God's great intention for mankind and for every Christian. Anything less leads to emptiness and a feeling of utter dissatisfaction. When God's people were in Egypt, they were in bondage and became slaves. They were grovelling around on the earth. God wanted to teach them how to fly, but they preferred life on the ground. Just when they thought life had defeated them, God came and marched them out of Egypt across the Red Sea into the Promised Land. "You have seen what I did unto the Egyptians and how I bare you on eagles' wings and brought you unto myself" (Exodus 19:4).

When I consider how God reached the orphan children in our care, it still touches my heart. Many of them had no hope in the world, yet Christ rescued and redeemed them. He set them free from their past and gave them a future.

When I recall some of their dirty little faces and dishevelled clothing when they arrived at our home and then compare this with the incredible transformation we witnessed in their lives it convinces me more than anything that God wants the best for His children. Their faces were always washed, their hairs combed, their dress immaculate and even their table manners and general social graces had improved. The biggest change, however, in many of the children, was in their attitude towards Louise and I and others. This came due to what is termed "The new birth". Many of the children had trusted God and Christ as their Saviour and it showed. The sadness was replaced with smiles. The lack of cooperation soon turned into a desire to help others and a reluctance to think of self. Even in our little church, they couldn't wait to play piano, guitar, drums or some other instrument. A choir was formed and they would not only sing, but look like angels every Sunday, although we knew otherwise! During the week these children were still children. They still had their moments, but how God had looked upon them and brought such a change to their lives! He'd literally lifted them from the gutter of life and from a state of homelessness and fear, offering them instead a future in Him. The Bible says of God's great love "Are not two sparrows sold for a penny and yet not one of them will fall to the ground without your Father's permission" (Matthew 10:29). His eye is upon the sparrow, the widow and the orphan child, the poor and the penniless. His eye is upon the bereaved, the broken-hearted, the disappointed and the destitute. His eye is upon the sinner who feels trapped in a cycle of defeat. It doesn't matter what prison cell you are currently in today, Jesus has the key to unlock the door and pave the way for your recovery. God's desire is to unlock the prison door, to see us sprint into the joys of life and, not just the joys of this life, but the wonders of the life to come. To quote a well know hymn "There was no other good enough to pay the price of sin, He only could unlock the gate of heaven and let us in"

Just as I would come home and set Snowbell free from his own little prison, Christ has also promised to set the captive free. He alone is the key to our future. Jesus said "I am the door, if anyone enters in by me, he shall be saved and shall go in and out and find pasture"(John 10:9). In the book of John He adds "Whom the Son sets free is free indeed" (John 8:36) and again in the book of Luke Jesus declared "The Spirit of the Lord is upon me because He has anointed me to preach the gospel to the poor, He has sent me to heal the broken-hearted, to proclaim release to the captives, and recovery of sight to the blind, and to set free those who are oppressed" (Luke 4:18). Paul exhorts "Looking unto Jesus, the author and finisher of our faith". Christians should aim high because God wants them to learn to fly. If you are a Christian and you've been spending more of your time and energy on earthly things; then learn to fly, learn to run and grace the mountains.

With Christ any prison door can be unlocked. The sky is the limit in terms of what we can achieve in this life. Jesus Himself said "With men things are impossible, but with God all things are possible to those who believe" (Matthew 19:26). We can walk, even run upon the mountains of this life, but not until Christ first unlocks the door.

It is such knowledge that helps many believers rise from the ashes of defeat and disappointment. They know that God has a greater plan for their lives and He alone has the power to deliver them from every set-back. Even ministers go through similar periods caused by horrific events during their service. Some quit and never return to God's ministry; others, by God's good grace, hang in and wait and see what God will do. They wait to allow God to maximise their potential, for our seemingly past failures are often used by God to prepare us for a successful future. In short, they believe they are born to run.

During those ferocious early years in Romania, we had been left quite traumatised. For the first time in my life personal dreams had literally died and I admit I considered quitting. I hid in our apartment under a cloud of grief. True, self-pity was probably the root cause of this. Like Elijah the prophet in the book of Kings, who lay under a juniper tree and preferred to die rather than live, I too felt quite hopeless. Regardless of many other notable achievements in Romania, I couldn't help feeling like an abject failure and, unusually for me, I started to become a bit of a recluse. They say memory is more binding than injustice and gradually I understood this quotation all too well. No matter how hard I tried I just couldn't shake off the things that had happened to us in Romania and my self-esteem dropped to an all-time low. Cynical, sad and depressed I was desperately upset and unhappy. My body, too, was stressed out and I felt very unwell. It was imperative to shield these destructive and negative emotions from the children, which was no mean task. This was equally important every time I entered our church. I was extremely conscious that people needed to hear good news, not my tales of woe, so I found myself "performing" for an hour and a half, before returning to what had become my own self-made prison cell inside our home. These were some of the loneliest, most miserable and troublesome days of my life; a period of total darkness I thought would never end, but everyone goes through periods of darkness and, trusting in God, we can also make it through such places of darkness. Even history itself records prodigious days of darkness such as when darkness fell upon the land of Egypt, a darkness the book of Exodus says could be felt. While Jesus, too, was on the cross we are told that from the sixth hour until the ninth hour darkness was over all the land. Even at creation, God separated the light from the darkness calling the light day and the darkness night. In a spiritual sense we, too, were not immune from our own night-time experience, but out of our own darkness greater light emerged. The arrival of Snowbell introduced the beginning of a new, more pleasant time in Romania and beyond and, with God's help we all began to run again over the mountains of life. As I took exercise with my dog I could feel the promptings of the Holy Spirit say to my soul "You can overcome defeat, depression and revulsion. You can learn to love again, trust again and believe again; you can learn to sing again and run again". I recalled a well-known chorus "On mountains high I'll praise your name in valleys low I'll do the same, as the river runs to find the ocean blue, my heart will always run to find you". Have you been hurt? Are you broke, busted and disgusted? Have you been left disappointed at life? God is waiting to heal those wounds

A group of Mexican distance runners known as the running people have a saying "When you run on the earth and with the earth, you can run forever". That's how I used to feel in my youth during my athletic training runs though Castle Park, close to my home in Bangor, Co Down. As I glided through the park, in peak condition, I was at one with God and God with me. The joy of being in great shape and communing with God at the same time is still something I can't properly explain. In those moments, I felt I could achieve anything.

In our world it's easy to become so disillusioned due to the setbacks many people encounter, but Christ said "All things are possible to those who believe" (Matthew 19:16). He didn't say "some things". Instead He made it clear that "all things" are possible with God.

Is there anything worse than seeing someone who has wonderful potential unable to use it because he or she is locked up in a prison of unbelief, ill-health, disobedience and even sin? This is Satan's plan and purpose, of course, to shackle and hinder many from hitting the heights which God intended for our lives. The book of John tells us that "the thief", who is Satan, "comes not but for to steal, kill and to destroy", but Jesus said "I am come that you might have life and have it more abundantly" (John 10:10).

Life is tough these days. Unemployment, recession and even apostasy is rampant inside and outside the church. Even many seemingly strong Christians are so discouraged they have literally given up on their dreams. They just sit at home all day and accomplish little for God, themselves and their families. This is not God's best intention for you.

I once titled a sermon I prepared and preached in Romania: "Get up, go on, be strong, it won't be long". The sermon looked at how God rebuked the children of Israel for mourning too long for Moses. He gave them thirty days to grieve, then said "Moses my servant is dead, now therefore arise, go over this Jordan thou and this entire people, unto the land which I do give to them and to the children of Israel" (Joshua 2:9). God wanted to take His people to the Promised Land, a land flowing with milk and honey; yet in order to possess it they had to learn to trust a new leader, Joshua, and leave behind the life they once knew under the direction of the great prophet Moses.

God is on the mountaintop and in the valleys. God was on the mountaintop with Moses in all of His majesty as He gave us the 10 commandments and God was down in the valley with Israel and its sin. God was on the mountaintop with David as fear engulfed Israel when they faced the Philistines, and down in the valley with Goliath's threats when God anointed David to defeat the giant. God is a God of the future, not just of the past. He longs for us to get up and move on even from ghastly things which have afflicted our lives. That's why He told Joshua three times to "be strong and of good courage". His best for us is not to see us sitting at the graveside of things which have long since passed away, but instead to be full of life and vigour for His honour and glory.

Paul rebuked the church of his own generation for succumbing to negative situations, but if Paul was upset that his brethren were not fulfilling their God-given assignments and potential, how much more was God saddened? The purpose of God for every child of His is that we might run well and experience a victorious life, even during times of persecution. Jeremiah the prophet illustrates this with the words "For I know the thoughts I think towards you, thoughts of peace and not of evil, to give you an expected end" (Jeremiah 29:11). These words were not written to people on the mountain-top, but to people in exile and in the valley of great persecution; nevertheless God's purpose for their lives was still a grand one, destined never to fail.

God's mountain-top men and women have a bright future and are going somewhere. It's not His intention to lock up His children and watch them waste their lives—that's the work of the enemy. He always wants us to glare back at the place where we assume we failed, but when we replay the past, we poison our future. Refuse to focus on where you've been and start heading for where you can be. The past has nothing new to say about your future. Remember, men do and will fail, but the great ones get back up again. Get up, go on, and be strong because it won't be long until we ourselves reach the Promised Land.

If you don't think you were born to run; you're not only denying history; you're denying who you really are", said Dennis Bramble. Unquestionably the child of God is born to grace the mountains, born to soar like the eagle, born to run, run and keep on running . . . . so get back out there and experience everything God has for you.

CHAPTER SIX

HE LOVED CHILDREN AND CHILDREN LOVED HIM!

"Suffer the little children to come unto me, and forbid them
not, for of such is the Kingdom of God" (Mark 10:13-14).

LESSON 6—TAKING A STAND FOR CHILDREN IS NOT FOR THE FAINT-HEARTED.

Most pastors will admit that getting people to come to church isn't always easy, but every Sunday morning I could always count on my first convert to arrive long before the rest—Snowbell. The reason he loved these Sunday services so much was due to the busloads of young people who would regularly travel from the city of Timisoara to attend our meetings and to lavish him with attention. Add to this his normal play-time with the children in our own home afterwards and, as far as Snowbell was concerned, church was the only place to be; in fact Sunday appeared to be his favourite day of the week.

Snowbell was referred to by the villagers as the "Pentecostal dog", especially when he stood outside to greet the bus as it pulled up in front of the church. He just loved to play with these young people and with our own children and they loved to play with him. I can still see him parading up and down in anticipation of the bus arriving.

One Sunday morning he decided to join me on the platform at the close of our service. The side door of the church was blown open by the wind and, wouldn't you know it, Snowbell seized his opportunity to come inside and see what was going on. As he sat right at the front of the church, all of us burst out laughing and, when I announced him as my new assistant pastor, the younger children certainly saw the funny side of this incident. On another Sunday, however, I was locking up when I noticed Snowbell happily surrounded by many of our children until they were rudely interrupted by the security man. Running into the middle of them, he leaned over, lifted the dog and proceeded to put him inside his hut. The children were upset, but not half as upset as the dog. He began barking in real 'Snowbell style' disapproval. The security man was clearly fed up with all the noise and commotion that was taking place that afternoon, although the kids appeared to be having the time of their lives, so, too, the dog. At that moment I felt sorry for them all. Immediately I asked the security man why he had removed Snowbell from the children. After all, they were enjoying playing with their favourite dog and he was clearly in his element playing with them. Besides, as Sunday dinner was being prepared, it was an excellent way of entertaining the children who, if left alone to do their own thing, certainly knew how to get up to plenty of mischief. "Bring the dog back out again" I demanded, which brought loud cheers of delight from the little ones. "He's not doing any harm and the children are enjoying playing with him," I assured the security man. Sure enough, as soon as the dog came back out, he was wagging his tail furiously and jumping up and down all over the children. Smiles had also returned to their little faces and all was well with the world again.

It's easy to dismiss children, in the same way that our guard lost his patience that day with them and the dog. Children require so much work and let's be honest, they continually make mistakes and need help. It's so easy to be negative about children, yet the Lord Jesus views them very differently. In one of the most intriguing New Testament stories Jesus is prevented from being with little children by, of all people, His own apostles. This in turn upset the Lord greatly so He told the disciples that His followers must never stop children from coming to know Him. The book of Mark says: "And they brought young children to Him, that He should touch them, and His disciples rebuked those who brought them. But when Jesus saw it, He was much displeased and said unto them: "Suffer the little children to come unto me, and forbid them not, for of such is the Kingdom of God" (Mark 10:13-14). Jesus has a tremendous love for children and is as concerned about them just as much as He is about any adult man or woman. Many of His miracles were actually performed on children. The New Testament records how Christ once delivered a demon-possessed boy, healed a nobleman's son, and raised from the dead a little girl and a widow's son in the city of Nain. It's also significant that Christ was never reluctant to hold or touch a child, love a child or perform a miracle on behalf of a child. Sadly we live in days when even parents are afraid to express love towards their own children for fear of being accused of inappropriate behaviour. Even to find a child who is lost and alone these days is a precarious situation to be in as immediately the finder becomes a prime suspect regarding abduction. In Bible days children had little or no rights. Once they matured they were also expected to work like an adult. This all changed when Jesus stood up to His very own followers. He became their champion spokesperson and their defender. By rebuking His own disciples, Christ demonstrated just how important children are to God. Of course, the need to stand up for children is just as great today as it was then. Working for God, with and on behalf of children, is not only a great privilege; it's the very heart of God Himself. Whether we teach Sunday school, or weekly children's activities or even playschool and primary age, God has given us a great task—the task of not only educating children but also protecting them.

At times I felt more like a lawyer in Romania than a pastor, given the amount of legal work I ended up having to do in relation to genuine child protection issues. I would often ask "What would Jesus do when faced with taking a stand for, and on behalf of children?" The answer was always the same "Suffer the little children to come unto me for of such is the Kingdom of God". Jesus loved children and children loved Him. He always defended them from immoral men. And God's miraculous power to save, heal and rescue children is still available today.

For various reasons children in Romania were at great risk during our time there. Our decision to oppose in particular, the lack of familiarisation period experienced by Romanian children with prospective parents before being adopted brought a level of intimidation I was not expecting and portrayed for me a very concerning picture of just how deep-rooted crime involving the exploitation of children really is. I learned that taking a stand for children is not for the faint-hearted.

My first eye-opener, if you like, into the seedy world of child-trafficking came as I was going about my normal business during my first year in Romania. Having made the decision to contest the local authorities on the issue of inappropriate adoptions of children, which included numerous appearances in Romanian courts, constant efforts were made to try and get us to desist from our legal campaign, the most aggressive of which took place right under the noses of every-day Romanian citizens. "You have one week to get out of our country", insisted the roughly spoken Romanian man. Assisted by his powerfully built companions this individual had me pinned against the wall of the Romanian national bank in Timisoara. I had gone there to perform our weekly transaction for the Children's House never imagining, of course, what was about to transpire. They were intimidating characters resembling professional weight lifters and, given my own light frame, had little trouble lifting me. In broad daylight, as customers were streaming in and out of the bank, I felt the full force of a fist firing firmly into my ribs. Instantly I realised this was not a game I was involved in. After a few, sharp, intakes of breath, mercifully the men disappeared almost as quickly as they'd arrived. Meanwhile I was left shaking. Of course, I ought to have been used to bullying of this sort. Having been brought up in Northern Ireland during the period known as "the Troubles" when over three thousand people lost their lives from the early 1970's to the late 1990's, paramilitary groups regularly ordered people out of our own country. Yet it took me to go to the land of Romania to experience for myself the full extent of such a frightening incident. Naturally I didn't sleep very well following the confrontation and fear continued to stalk me for weeks, even months afterwards. My life had been threatened and I needed to take that threat seriously.

Another incident brought home to me just how serious these matters were. Attending a Christmas function in Bucharest, organised by legal representatives, I was enjoying mingling with the great and the good of Romania, when one leading Romanian lawyer quickly had me choking on my food. Taking a sip from his wine glass, he looked over his designer spectacles and casually warned me that our fight was not only with well organised criminals, but with people involved in a multi-million dollar industry—the trafficking of vulnerable children. "I admire what you're doing, but if you've any sense, stay well clear of it", he told me. His offer was very tempting. After all, I didn't need this hassle. I'd come to help run a children's house and look after a village church. That was much easier and much less threatening. Besides people at home and in Romania would understand if we backed down. There were other, more equipped professionals such as the police and government public figures whose job it was to sort this problem out. I was a pastor and I had other justifiable duties to carry out. Yet again, however, I heard in my spirit a voice I would hear many times in Romania with regard to the fight on behalf of children. The voice simply whispered "What would Jesus do?" I may have been just a local pastor, but in the eyes of many of the children I was their father, the only father some of them had. So, with God's help and grace, I received the courage to reject any notion to abandon our campaign. Whether I liked it or not God had placed a massive responsibility on me to help protect the innocents and it was to Him I would ultimately be accountable. There was no going back. Into His hands I committed our cause and my spirit. I was still scared stiff, like David in the Old Testament who, despite showing courage in taking on Goliath, would still have no doubt been petrified at such a prospect. Sometimes it's easy to look at our opponents and see them as too big, too difficult, and even impossible to overcome. But just as God enabled a little shepherd boy called David, a youth, no less, to topple a Philistine giant with just a single sling shot, so too, God uses the weak things of our world to bring down the high and mighty and corrupt of this world.

The responsibility for children today is patently obvious as child protection measures have tightened considerably and for good reasons. We live in a world where children are regularly being abused; therefore the call for Christian workers to help children has never been greater. It's so hard to comprehend that many adults do not have the best interests of children at heart. When we first arrived in Romania I believed it was with the purpose of shepherding a church and taking care of the daily needs of children, but clearly what transpired was totally beyond my wildest imagination. Ours was a daily battle to protect children from the deceitful schemes of people who clearly had little or no regard for their welfare.

These unscrupulous individuals instead used children as "political footballs" and sought to prosper financially from their misfortune. Romanian courtrooms were full of cases of children being targeted for international adoption or cited for an adoption that clearly was not beneficial to the child. The advice given to me by that lawyer in Bucharest only really hit home when I was required to defend children in courts in Bucharest and in other parts of Europe, where adoptions like these were commonplace and on a daily basis. I realised then we were caught up in something satanic and deeply disturbing. I was surprised at the level of anger I experienced, too, a righteous anger that wanted to object constantly about this problem. What had happened to me? I used to consider myself a quiet, peaceful person, regularly able to contain my emotions. Instead, rapidly I became both angry and astonished at the complacency which seemed to exist regarding the exploitation of children in Romania and I readily confess that I blew my top on more than one occasion. Initially I was grieved at how angry I'd grown at the authorities. I continually felt like I had let the Lord down, but later learned this was just the voice of the enemy. In time, God showed me that such anger is permitted in order to bring justice to suffering children. Righteous anger is something which is perfectly acceptable in order to protect the most vulnerable in our society, especially children. Anger has been described as the birthplace for solutions. There comes a time when "enough is enough" and when being angry is not just necessary, it is biblically acceptable. Righteous anger helps set the captives free. Moses continually displayed righteous anger at Pharaoh in the book of Exodus with the statement "Let my people go". The Bible tells us to "be angry and sin not". Righteous anger is healthy and was exactly what Christ demonstrated when he overturned the tables of the thieves and money changers and rebuked His disciples for sending children away. The Bible says that Jesus went into the temple of God and cast out all them that sold and bought in the temple, and overthrew the tables of the moneychangers and the seats of them that sold doves. Then we see righteous anger as Christ announces "My house shall be called the house of prayer, but you have made it a den of thieves" (Matthew 21:12-13).

What happens, however, when we are prevented from helping or saving children from abuse? What transpires when we did all that we could, but evil appears to have triumphed? I readily admit that we didn't win every battle in Romania. Many times it grieved me that despite our best efforts, we seemingly failed to prevent other incidents of child exploitation. Thankfully when this occurs, there's another court of appeal, the highest court of all, for God Himself will take His own vengeance on those who harm children and He will ultimately protect them. The Bible tells us that "Though my father and mother forsake me, the Lord will take me up" (Psalm 27:10).

Often I exploded at the blatant injustices in Romania. Despite the fact that our home had been running very well and the children were developing nicely, we were regularly being summoned to the offices of the Child Protection to answer questions which we felt were clearly unnecessary and totally provocative in relation to the subject of religion. These were trivial meetings, but very explosive. One day, much to the surprise of the Child Protection, things did not go according to plan. Arriving with both my secretary and translator, we were made to wait for hours at the end of a long line of people, nothing unusual in Romania, before being shown into a dark intimidating room. It was hot and sticky and reminded me of one of those old industrial type buildings, a scene from a World War 2 movie. The officials were seated at one end of the room and we were shown to our seats at the opposite end. In between there was enough space to hold a football match. The scene resembled the atmosphere of an office belonging to a grumpy headmaster and produced a fear factor similar to a dentist's or doctor's surgery. Then the administrative firing squad began questioning us in a most patronising manner. They had clearly been waiting for us and had prepared for us. Their unfriendly demeanour made us feel like we were in a police station being questioned about a serious crime, rather than what was supposed to have been a routine child protection meeting. It became clear to me that we were not only being intimidated and mocked; our time and efforts were also being totally disrespected by insensitive bureaucrats. Something snapped inside me. I was tired and frustrated and had literally taken enough. Uncharacteristically I banged the table as hard as I could, pushed my chair across the room and began telling those opposite us what I really thought of them. In my rage, of course, I reminded these people that neither I, nor my wife, needed to be in Romania and that we had come to be a blessing to their nation and children. I reminded them of the cost regarding the building of our home which had been funded exclusively by our own church and built by our own members. Finally I told them we were leaving and to never again treat me or our organisation with such contempt. It was a bold step and I was afraid I had overstepped the mark. I even considered the fact that I may have fractured our relationship to the point of no return. I envisaged phoning and booking a couple of one-way plane tickets for us both home to Ireland. Surprisingly, however, from that day forward we were treated very differently; it was as though I had earned the respect of the local authorities and to our amazement they never again called us back to such a meeting. What transpired taught me a pivotal lesson in life, namely "What we tolerate we cannot change". This applies to every area of our lives for if we accept sinful practices they will only increase.

We must challenge evil and take a stand against it. There are people who boast of having no enemies anywhere in the world. Do you know why? Because they have never taken a stand for anything! They have never understood what it is to sacrifice or cost them something. "You have an enemy? That is good. It means you have stood up for something some time in your life" Winston Churchill once commented. Do not, however, stand alone. Paul says "Wherefore take unto you the whole armour of God, that ye may be able to withstand in the evil day, and having done all to stand, stand therefore"(Ephesians 6:13). While we are subject to authority, we must never allow others to humiliate us and rob us of our self-respect. A Christian serves a higher authority, one which is fair and balanced, not totalitarian or tyrannical. We would require this anger and mettle on many more occasions during our time in Romania, mixed, of course, with God's great measure of grace which comes exclusively through Jesus Christ his Son. It was tiring and stressful work, a difficult balance to achieve, but God blessed every endeavour.

From the time of our arrival, it felt like Satan himself had unleashed the forces of hell against us to try and hinder everything we attempted to do; notwithstanding we still managed to obtain many objectives, not least our priority to help stem the tide of illegal international adoption. Due to countless appearances in courtrooms throughout the length and breadth of the land, between 2001 and 2006, particularly Timisoara and Bucharest, our team ultimately managed to play a defining role in bringing to the attention of the government the sheer size of the problem regarding the illegal international adoption of children there.

We were ecstatic when a new government passed a law, supported by the EU, giving children in Romania the right to "satisfactory familiarisation period" with prospective parents, something which was desperately required. World vision reported that illegal adoption is a contributing factor to child trafficking. The report, 10 things you need to know about human trafficking, warns of situations in which desperation and vulnerability may lead to parties overlooking both the new law and child rights in the adoption process. To circumvent those systems sets a dangerous precedent that can ultimately contribute to child trafficking. We had helped slay our own Goliath and succeeded in helping to protect some of the vulnerable. Our efforts would ultimately, even if unexpectedly, be commended in writing by the new government of Romania for the role we had played in this nationwide child protective measure, a gesture which was most appreciated. For this achievement alone it was worth those intense, but rewarding years we had endured—years which were brutal and destructive to our lives, but years which had taught me a powerful lesson; taking a stand for children is certainly not for the faint-hearted.

Chapter Seven

<hr/>

Miracle dog; Miracle God

"The Spirit of the Lord is upon me, for He has anointed me
to preach the gospel to the poor, He hath sent me to heal the
broken-hearted, to preach deliverance to the captives and
recovering of sight to the blind, to set at liberty those that are
broken" (Luke 4:18)

Lesson 7—God is a miracle-working God.

The Labrador and their first crosses with Golden Retrievers are now thought to be the most commonly used breed working as guide dogs in the United Kingdom. Initially I was totally unaware of this innate ability which Snowbell so obviously possessed. As far as I was concerned Snowbell was just a dog and nothing more. How wrong I was and how utterly ignorant regarding his remarkable all round abilities! As stated earlier, these dogs assist the blind, the disabled and even the police at airports as they seek out prohibited drugs. This breed of dog has an acute sense of smell thus enabling it to pick up the minutest traces of the scent of drugs such as cannabis, heroin and amphetamines. This sense of smell is said to be many times more sensitive than that of humans. Dogs like Snowbell have aptly been described as scent machines. All dogs possess this amazing sense of smell, but especially Labradors. For instance, so phenomenal are these dogs they can alert their diabetic owners that a hypoglycacmic attack is coming, because they can smell the subtle body odour that means blood sugar is low. Likewise they can tell when we are anxious because the smell of our sweat is different when we are worried. They live in a world of smell, not sight. It astonished me to learn that so great are a Labradors own attributes in this department that gangs in the United States have even been known to put out "contracts" to kill dogs that have found millions of dollars worth of drugs. These dogs can also comfort those suffering from PTSD (Post Traumatic Stress Disorder), they can smell cancers, and even sense when an epileptic is about to have a seizure.

I still fondly recall an incident which occurred to me while at Heathrow Airport in London a few years ago on my way back to Romania. Rushing for a flight, I happened to notice a camera crew hurrying towards me. "Why do they wish to interview me?" was my initial thought. "Maybe there is a major celebrity standing behind me" followed a more realistic explanation. Immediately turning round, however, there was a celebrity, the most beautiful Labrador waiting and posing gracefully for those same cameras. He clearly loved every minute of it. If ever anyone was made for "lights, camera, action" it was him. Airport security police were also there, armed with machine guns. "Is everything alright", I enquired. "Everything's fine, they are just doing a story on my dog," replied the officer. "Why would the press make such a fuss of one little dog" I said. I never forgot his reply. "Because he's a miracle dog," responded the proud officer. What this policeman clearly meant was that his guide dog was highly trained in various fields and could at times perform miracles in helping change the lives of many individuals. I for one can vouch for that now. When Snowbell entered our own lives and our home we were totally discouraged, however, slowly but surely, Snowbell's innate miracle working powers began to surface. Subtly he managed to get me to accept him, become fascinated by him, before finally coming to love him. This soft, cuddly, crafty little Labrador made us all smile again and took away the pain of the past and excited me about the future. I can understand more now why these dogs can even act as mobility aid to the blind and visually impaired. They provide freedom and independence as well as being a faithful and loving companion. With the increased mobility and independence gained through the use of a guide dog, the confidence of the blind or visually impaired person soars. Well trained guide dogs stand out because of their alertness and intelligence and their willingness to serve. This training apparently takes between two and five years to accomplish.

Once the training is complete, however, the dog can be fully trusted to give sight back to the blind, to meet the needs of a disabled person and to help find those narcotics that would previously have been impossible to trace. But that's not the end of their miraculous attributes. Dogs in general have a powerful sense of touch and a sixth sense, often anticipating events before they happen. They are also able to miraculously trace their way home from a distant destination. There's a famous movie entitled "Red Dog". It tells the incredible story of a dog's love for its master. Red dog became an Australian legend when, after the sudden death of her owner who was killed in a car crash and not found for days, the dog went in search of its master. After tracking half way across Australia, the dog eventually managed to not only find its own way home, but position itself at the very graveside of its now buried owner. Yes, Red Dog did all of this without the use of Sat Nav or even Google maps!

The intelligence of these amazing dogs has so far been put down to trainability. Nevertheless, the more scientists study dogs, the more remarkable they find them to be. Take the dogs from Canine Partners, a charity that trains dogs to help people with disability. These dogs can press an alarm button to get an ambulance, help with dressing and undressing and get money out of the hole in the wall. They can empty the washing machine and do about 200 other tasks and even receive a carer's allowance! And what about Red the lurcher who learned to open his cage at Battersea Dogs Home a few years back? He didn't just escape on his own. He would let out as many as nine other dogs he was friendly with. Then they would all play and steal whatever food was available.

Labradors themselves are not just intelligent and efficient working with the blind, however. They can also be trained to work with deaf people and this is another area where these dogs are improving the quality of the lives of their owners. I once watched a programme about a Labrador that was so skilled and trained he even knew how to pull the socks off his disabled owner each night before she went to bed. Even Snowbell would never respond to the sound of any bus other than the one belonging to our home. He couldn't see the bus when it approached the house due to the large gates which protected the home, but he could clearly hear it. All buses sounded the same to me, but not to Snowbell. As soon as our driver would turn the bus around the corner to arrive home, Snowbell would immediately sprint towards the door to greet the children and Louise. He was a miracle dog in so many ways. Dogs can apparently hear sound at four times the distance humans can. No one illustrates this difference better than Michael Hingson, whose dog Roselle helped him escape from the World Trade Centre disaster in New York back in 2001. Hingson wrote in his excellent book, Thunder Dog, "If I can hear things happening twenty steps below, she can clearly hear what's going on 80 steps below". Without Roselle he claims he would never have made it out alive.

A trained hearing dog will alert a deaf person to a variety of household sounds. This can include alarm clocks, the door bell, cooker timer and specially adapted phones for the deaf. The dog will touch the owner when he hears the sound. They are also trained to respond to the sounds of fire or smoke alarms indicating there is an emergency. You may be able to hide your emotions from another human, but you cannot hide them from your dog—especially a Labrador retriever. He has instincts which are almost supernatural.

It's the same with the Son of God. Just as Labradors are sent to aid the blind person physically, Jesus Christ has been sent to give sight to the spiritually blind of this world. We cannot run or hide anything from Him. The Psalmist said "If I ascend up into heaven you are there and if I make my bed in hell, behold you are there" (Psalm 139:8). God, who knows our every thought, opens the eyes of the spiritually blind person, helping them to see the love of God through Jesus Christ His Son. To not see God is to not see Jesus who is the Son of the living God. When the scribes and Pharisees accused Jesus of being possessed with a devil, the people responded saying: "These are not the words of one that hath a devil, can the devil open the eyes of the blind?" Jesus said of the spiritually blind, "This is why I speak to them in parables, because seeing they do not see and hearing they do not hear, nor do they understand" (Matthew 13:13). The purpose of this book is to open many eyes to God's great love for them through the help of parables and stories. We need God to open our eyes because the Bible tells that "the god of this world has blinded the minds of unbelievers to keep them from seeing the gospel of light of the glory of Christ who is the image of God". (2 Corinthians 4:4). Michael W. Smith wrote: "Open the eyes of my heart, Lord, open the eyes of my heart, I want to see you". Satan is the god of this world and, as Jesus tells us in

John chapter twelve, "he has blinded the eyes of unbelievers and hardened their heart, lest they see with their eyes, and understand with their heart, and turn, and I would heal them" (John 12:40). Once God opens the eyes of the unbeliever immediately they get a glimpse of the glory of God and the exalted Christ and light begins to shine again. Jesus restored the sight of a blind man who used to sit and beg, but only after he was willing to receive help. The first step to gain our spiritual sight is to acknowledge that we are blind and then become willing to let God open our eyes to see as He sees. When others disputed what had happened to the blind man, he simply replied, "One thing I do know, once I was blind, but now I see" (John 9:25). By the grace and mercy of our Lord Jesus Christ the blind man's eyes were restored to see this beautiful world.

I recall attending a media conference which highlighted expressively what it must be like to be physically or spiritually blind. The conference was held by media consultant and author of several well-known Christian books, Phil Cooke. He played a video which showed a blind man sitting with a begging bowl on the street. The man had a sign beside the bowl which read "I'm blind, please give generously". Hundreds of people passed this man, but very few stopped to ask how he was or indeed to donate much money. Observing all of this was a young girl whose arrival on the scene radically changed the situation for the blind man. She noticed how no one was giving and boldly asked the man if she could change the wording on his sign. After he agreed, she then proceeded to write the words "It's a beautiful day, but I can't see it". Instantly the man could hear the increase in money being given to him as practically every person who passed him dropped something into his little offering basket. Of course, the purpose of this video was to demonstrate the power of words and highlight how best to write advertising slogans or get a message across. Nevertheless, for me, it clearly highlighted what it must be like to be not only physically blind, but spiritually blind also. There are millions of people living without Christ who, because of their blindness, miss the beauty of each day with God. It's a beautiful day out there with God, but they can't see it.

Spiritual blindness is more serious than physical blindness because we remain guilty of our sins and become the object of God's wrath. Jesus Christ not only came to give sight to the blind, but to open the ears of the spiritually deaf, to help the spiritually disabled and to cleanse the world of sin and crime. In one of His most powerful New Testament statements Jesus is recorded as saying in the book of Luke, "The Spirit of the Lord is upon me, for He has anointed me to preach the gospel to the poor, He hath sent me to heal the broken-hearted, to preach deliverance to the captives and recovering of sight to the blind, to set at liberty those that are broken" (Luke 4:18). In other words Christ is a miracle-working God who not only opens the eyes of the blind physically, as he proved while on the earth performing many miracles, but more significant is the fact that He helps the spiritually impaired and deaf also. Writing about Christ's coming, the prophet Isaiah said: "And in that day shall the deaf hear the words of the book and the eyes of the blind shall see out of obscurity and out of darkness". The Lord Jesus came to meet our every need. He came to provide for the poor, heal the most broken of hearts, and deliver those chained to addictions of every kind" (Isaiah 29:18).

This Creator God who through the shedding of His precious blood at Calvary and His wonderful resurrection and ascension can change the lives of countless millions. There is literally nothing too hard for the Lord, His love reaches into every part of society. "The Lord gives sight to the blind, he lifts up those who are bowed down, and the Lord loves the righteous" (Psalm 146:8).

The Bible records the astonishing miracles of God in both the Old and New Testaments. In the Old Testament we read of the miracle of creation and of the miracles performed by Moses, Elijah and Elisha. Then the Bible describes at least 39 miracles in the New Testament which Jesus performed during his public ministry and various other miracles associated with Him, such as His birth, transfiguration, resurrection and ascension. Christ opened the eyes of the blind, healed lepers and paralytics, healed men and women of various illnesses, performed exorcisms, raised the dead and even performed miracles over nature by calming the wind and the waves, turning water into wine and feeding the 5,000.

We are told of Christ's supernatural abilities "And Jesus went about all Galilee teaching in their synagogues and preaching the gospel of the kingdom and healing all manner of sickness and all manner of disease among the people. And his fame went throughout all Syria and they brought unto him all sick people that were taken with divers diseases and torments and those which were possessed with devils and those which were lunatic and those that had palsy and he healed them"(Matthew 4 23-24). With such biblical proof regarding Christ's miraculous life, especially in relation to His resurrection, why do people still reject God in their lives? Why do they walk in disobedience and in unbelief?

It is surely because they have no spiritual sight! The great philosopher, Albert Einstein, once said "there are only two ways to live your life. One is as though nothing is a miracle; the other is as though everything is a miracle". What do you see each day you get up? In Joel Osteen's book entitled "Your best life now" he says "It is our faith that activates the power of God". Ask God to open your eyes to miracles of nature and miracles of mercy all around you. Ask Him to reveal His greatness to you and He will.

Christ's miracles were even notably different in form. He displayed His power over nature, power over sickness, power to deliver and even His great power over death raising not just Himself from the grave but others such as Jairus's daughter, the widow of Nain's son and, of course, Lazarus. Thousands of books have been published presenting commentary on these various events, but even they cannot do justice to the miracles of Jesus.

In John chapter 2 we are informed about the first recorded miracle of Christ, but significantly there's no mention of His last recorded miracle. John penned in the final verse of his gospel "And there are also many other things which Jesus did, the which, if they should be written everyone, I suppose that even the world itself could not contain the books that should be written" (John 21:25). The supernatural ability of Christ is far beyond the ability of the greatest writer to explain.

I was struck by the heading on the Guide Dogs for The Blind Association web page which reads, "We will not rest until blind and partially sighted people can enjoy the same freedom of movement as others". As Christ went about healing the sick and all those who were oppressed of the devil, this was His motto too and it hasn't changed today. Even now He gives this sight to the blind and much more besides and He won't rest until lost people have been set totally free.

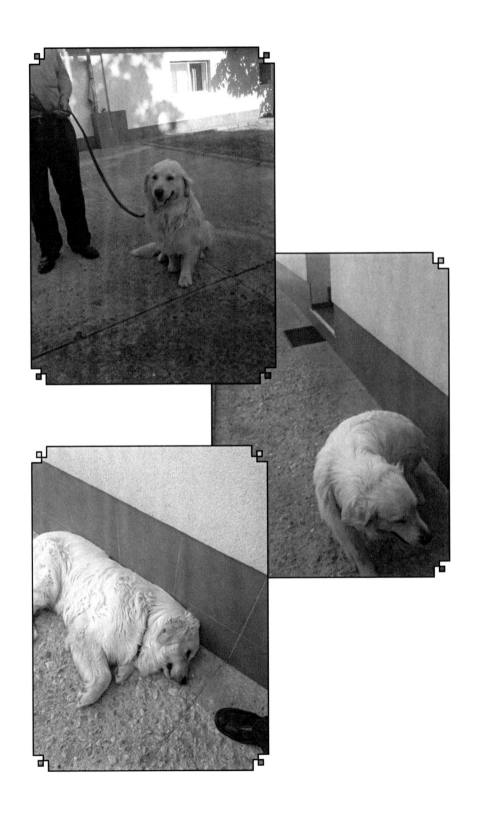

Chapter Eight

He Knew When He'd Done Wrong

"The wages of sin is death" (Romans 6:23).

Lesson 8—Even dogs have a built-in conscience.

We've all heard the expression "He's in the dog house" or "she's in the dog house". It's used, of course, in relation to an argument between couples in a relationship whereby one of them is 'in the wrong' and therefore metaphorically should be sleeping in 'the dog house', a small hut in the garden, rather than the couple's bed. Snowbell slept in a small building like this, but, of course, he didn't like being put there during the day. We would only insist on this if we were going out or if he'd been badly behaved. I still recall the very first time he ended up in the dog house for misbehaviour, due to an incident with my wife Louise. I still recall the ashen look on her face as she entered the living-room one evening following our weekly prayer meeting. She was literally "white as a sheet". Staring into space, Louise held the expression of someone who had just been given the most appalling news. "What's wrong, what's wrong?" I exclaimed. Louise didn't answer. Slowly, very slowly, she just kept on walking into the room, holding her stomach as if in excruciating pain. I knew there was a serious problem. I thought perhaps she had taken a telephone call informing her of a death in the family. I also considered the fact that maybe she had been verbally or physically assaulted by someone following the church service. "Please tell me, what happened?" I continued. She pointed to the window and muttered something about Snowbell. "Has he been knocked down and killed? Is he okay?" I asked, thinking, of course, that she had just seen our loving family pet taken from us. I soon realised that my wife was in severe shock and just couldn't respond.

Quickly I sat her down and ran outside to see just what had taken place. My secretary, Lacramioara, was still at the "scene of the crime" and even she looked more than a little bit dazed. "What happened here, Lacra?" I enquired. I was now becoming desperate for answers. Then I learned of Snowbell's first real misdemeanour, an error which at first made me feel incredibly angry. "Snowbell charged at Louise at full speed and knocked her down. She fell and lay on the ground for several minutes", declared Lacra. "Did she hit her head on the concrete?" was my first reaction. "Thankfully, no," replied Lacra who reckoned Louise was fortunate not to be even more injured than she actually was. My first instinct, of course, was to go after the dog and give him a right good telling off, maybe even a good spanking, even though I had never laid a hand on him previously. I was also aware of something I had read explaining how to discipline your dog when he does something wrong. It said that dogs do not respond to punishment, only to reward and non-reward. To beat one's dog is counter-productive and no matter how angry you feel, taking your frustrations out on your pet will not accomplish or change anything about the behaviour of your dog.

It was then, however, that Lacra mentioned something which settled my rage instantly. "Snowbell didn't mean it, Pastor John," she said. "He was so upset you can't imagine," she further pleaded in her familiar, but likable broken English. "You should have seen how he tucked in beside Louise as she lay upon the ground; it was as if he knew that he'd done wrong", she added. I realised then that the little dog had made his first major mistake in our home. I realised, too, that no matter how much I had come to love Snowbell—and even be fascinated with him—he wasn't perfect. I would love to portray that he was, but to be fair to this tale and even to the world in which we live, it's only right to note that during our incredible relationship Snowbell would not always do what he was told. Nevertheless, his reaction following the incident showed how much he'd grown to love Louise, who had become his daily companion. Normally he would wait for her coming down the stairs every morning for his breakfast, followed by a massage. He would even hold in his mouth a glove ready for her to stroke him with. Remarkably, however, the morning after the incident, Snowbell showed little or no interest in any such massage or even in his breakfast. Now there was a rare event! He would become distracted and at times unaware of just how grave the consequences of his wild behaviour could be towards those he loved.

His grieving didn't end there. We were amazed at how his entire behaviour altered over the next few days, even though my wife had already made a quite speedy recovery. He wouldn't eat and just seemed to sulk around the garden each day. We had to continually pat and stroke him and reassure him that everything was okay, but he wasn't convinced. He needed oceans of love, not condemnation for what he'd done. It seemed to us that he was clearly already well aware of the pain he had caused Louise and nothing we would convey to him about the incident could make him feel any better. It was as though he had his own "built in conscience".

Does this mean that he could differentiate between right and wrong? And, in a broader sense, do dogs in general know right from wrong? In Wild Justice: The Moral Lives of Animals, Marc Bekoff and his co-author, Jessica Pierce argue that dogs and other animals clearly display a sense of right and wrong and the moral sense of fairness and empathy. Although the book concentrates on animals in general, Bekoff and Pierce cite various examples relating to the behaviour of dogs. They mention a case of a larger, stronger male dog playing with a smaller, weaker male and restraining his bites so as to not injure the smaller dog. They also highlight the work of Friedericke Range and her colleagues in Austria, who have proved that dogs will refuse to work for food if they see that other dogs are getting more for doing the same thing. Bekoff and Peirce give a number of other examples, ranging from elephants to mice that conclusively show how animals have a sense of morality, compassion and a sense of right and wrong. Snowbell's behaviour after his reckless charge at Louise reminded me of our human state. We have what I would call a "built-in conscience" which tells us when we've done right or wrong. This conscience works regardless of whether people have made a decision to follow Christ or not. There's hardly a person on the planet who doesn't know the difference between right and wrong— an attribute not necessarily down to how we are raised from birth. On the contrary, it's God's computer system at work in all of our hearts to help lead us to Jesus and to a life of right living. Sometimes we are given instructions by our superiors and we know deep down such instructions are morally and ethically wrong. If we carry out these commands, of course, we then end up living with the guilt afterwards highlighted by our "built in conscience".

The Bible states that "righteousness exalts a nation, but sin is a reproach to any people"(Proverbs 13:24). We are further told by the apostle Paul that "the wages of sin is death" (Romans 6:23). Therefore doing the wrong thing will lead only to the wrong conclusion, not just in this life, but also in the life to come. God on the other hand wants us to follow our conscience and listen to what God through the Holy Spirit is saying to us about our daily behaviour. Paul writes in the book of Acts, "I do exercise myself to have always a conscience devoid of offence toward God and toward men" (Acts 24:16). Following some of King David's worst sins he made the following powerful statement: "Search me and know my heart, try me and know my thoughts, and see if there be any wicked way in me and lead me in the way everlasting" (Psalm 139:23-24). David probably already knew well what he had done wrong and so do we. The night Snowbell collided with Louise was a watershed night. It was a serious incident, yet good came out of it. It paved the way for us to train Snowbell not to do such a thing again. It helped us to start educating him in how to control his emotions and become a dog we could be proud of. It's hard to discipline those we love; nevertheless it's essential if any relationship is to continue as it should. It's been said that confrontation is just an attempt to save a relationship. We cannot correct what we are unwilling to confront. Snowbell was born for greatness and for higher service than a mere rascal running around the garden. In order to get him there discipline would now have to be administered and discipline is never pleasant. Phillip Keller writes, "The correction that comes with love causes pain, both for the administer and the recipient".

Many prefer to try and avoid discipline but God doesn't. When we have done wrong, the Lord will gently correct us in the same way that we are taught to correct our family dog. He will not punish us severely, as is often erroneously preached in pulpits throughout the land, but He will discipline us. God is not our enemy; He is our friend. He is not full of wrath, violence and hatred, but instead is filled with peace, mercy and love. His chief objective is to restore, not ruin or destroy. He takes away certain privileges and blessings until we see the error of our ways. He loves us too much to let us revert to a substandard life. Because He really cares, He corrects. If there is to be development then the saying holds true, "no pain, no gain!" The Bible says "For whom the Lord loves He chastens". The word chasten means discipline. We are further told "now chastening for the present seems not to be joyous, but grievous; nevertheless afterwards it yields the peaceable fruit of righteousness unto them which are exercised thereby" (Hebrews 12:11). God disciplines us merely to protect us because He loves us too much not to. It's proof of our adoption to Christ. His purpose is not to hurt us but to correct us and remind us that it is the blessing of God which makes us rich and adds no sorrow to our lives.

However, so that we understand how God works in relation to punishment when we sin, we first need to distinguish between punishment and discipline. If one is a believer in Jesus then all our past, present and future sins have already been paid for on the cross at Calvary. As Christians we will never again be punished for sin. This was done once, for all: as Paul writes "So Christ was once offered to bear the sins of many" (Hebrews 9:28). In other words as Paul also puts it "There is therefore now no condemnation for those who are in Christ Jesus, who walk not after the flesh, but after the spirit" (Romans 8:1).

It's sad when preachers condemn the body of Christ in the manner of a schoolmaster scolding his children for bad behaviour and fail to portray the true nature of God. The truth is God's people have been redeemed and forgiven of their sins. Believers are the recipients of mercy and grace, not punishment. Due to the awesome sacrifice of Christ, God sees only the righteousness of Christ when he looks at us. Our sin has been nailed to the cross with Jesus and we will never be punished for it.

Instead God brings His divine discipline to bear upon us when we continue to sin. If He did not, He would not be a loving and concerned Father. Just as we discipline our children for their welfare, so does our heavenly Father lovingly correct His children for their benefit.

It pained me to discipline Snowbell and our children, but it was something which had to be done. I remember once when one of the younger girls had misbehaved we took away some of her favourite treats, leaving her in tears. I was tempted to give in to her demands, after all, you know how manipulative little girls can be. She would roll her eyes, let a single tear fall and say "please, pastor John!" When that failed, she would quickly revert to telling me what a good dad I was and how beautiful my suit looked that particular day. Such manipulation nearly worked on numerous occasions, but to give in would only have proven counter-productive. This kind of discipline wouldn't last forever, either in the case of the children, or Snowbell. It was brief, yet necessary. Before long I was back reassuring the children and the dog that they were greatly loved. How similar is God's principle of discipline when we also go astray. I noticed a distinct change in many of the children following essential periods of disciple and in Snowbell after his "smash and grab act" upon Louise. He wasn't as excitable around her or me, or even others within the home. He genuinely appeared to learn his lesson and reformed his behaviour accordingly. Discipline then is how God lovingly turns His children from rebellion to obedience. Discipline affords us the opportunity to learn and conform ourselves to the image of Christ making it a good thing.

From the time of that incident, I have also learned that exhaustive studies have been undertaken to try and establish if dogs do experience guilt in this way. Science has taken on the big question of whether dogs really do feel guilt. Research from the Family Dog Project in Budapest, Hungary, the first research body dedicated to the relationship between dogs and humans, concludes that dogs are able to observe minute visible differences in the owner's behaviour and react to them. This may help explain the dogs act of contrition, just as Snowbell demonstrated after knocking Louise over onto the concrete. This contrition is apparently evident in dogs even before the owner is aware the dog has been a bad boy. The dog anticipates the owner's negative reaction to the misdemeanour so he apologises in advance, hoping for a pardon. Furthermore dogs are allegedly the only species showing this behaviour. They try to avoid punishment in the same way a man buys flowers for his wife when he knows he's displeased her in some way.

I recall another day when I returned home to the house only to find Snowbell squinty eyed, ears plastered and head bowed. Where have you been" I asked, as he hung his head in shame. A short walk into the kitchen soon gave me the answer as I noticed the bin re-arranged into a torn, chewed and sorted pile. He was guilty as charged and he looked every bit of it. Yet is this display of guilt shown by dog's simply doggie intuition or do they really feel bad after clattering their owners to the ground or leaving the kitchen in a mess? An experiment at Goldsmith College in London suggests that dogs show empathy and try to comfort people feeling emotional distress. Tested dogs approached and interacted not only with their owners, but also with a complete stranger who was crying. It would appear obvious then, that if a dog can feel sorry for someone else, surely he can feel sorry for his own actions and indeed for his wrong actions which have had a detrimental outcome on his owner? Guilt is a highly complex emotion that requires an understanding of a moral code, but that doesn't mean a dog can't understand forbidden behaviour. Dogs know after training what they can and cannot do and if they break the rules, guilt is written all over them.

New research reveals dogs and some other animals can experience so-called secondary emotions such as embarrassment, jealousy, empathy and guilt. Scientists know animal behaviour, but owners know their dogs and no research study is ever likely to convince pet owners that their grovelling dog isn't fully aware he was naughty, especially when chicken is stuck to his lip. Even the great observer of animal behaviour Konrad Luzenz wrote of the dog's "guilty look" saying "We can assume with certainty that every dog hides a guilty conscience". This was Snowbell, too. Remarkable as it occurred to us, it was as though this amazing little dog really did understand when he'd done wrong, but more amazingly he now seemed willing and ready to change in order to avoid the dog house.

CHAPTER NINE

BORN TO RETRIEVE

"For the Son of Man is come to seek and to save that which is lost". (Luke 19:10).

LESSON 9—GOD IS A RESTORING GOD.

Although initially I visualised Snowbell as an ideal family pet, it soon became clear to me that he, too, had many other marvellous attributes including the desire and ability to retrieve.

A most resilient dog, Labradors were originally required to work for many hours at a stretch retrieving game, both dead and wounded, to their handlers from both water and cover. Dr. Peter Neville writes "The retrieving instinct is a crucial aspect of the Labrador's character and should be borne in mind when choosing this breed". Dr. Neville points out how the Labrador is a natural retriever, a dog that always loves to carry items both around the home and when he's out on a walk. However, due care and attention needs to be given with regards to this instinctive behaviour or problems can arise for both dog and owner as I frequently found to my cost. For example, when we used to play in our little room indoors, Snowbell would constantly want to bring me something. We always kept toys in his room so he had something to fetch for us other than items which he shouldn't have had anywhere near his mouth, such as my freshly ironed shirt or my mobile phone which happened on several occasions. I was always so frightened in case he swallowed my phone; after all what would happen if it rang inside him? I even considered compiling a new voice mail saying—"Hi there, I can't take your call right now because my phone is inside my dog, however if you leave your name and number I will get back to you following my dog's operation!"

Snowbell possessed numerous attributes, but his greatest was the ability to retrieve. When outside Snowbell would grab other things like branches and carry them back to me with great pride. It's well known that these types of dogs never get bored when retrieving a ball, which is handy when it comes to tiring them out with exercise. Being a young dog, Snowbell had so much energy it was hard to keep him settled unless he expended that energy retrieving a multitude of things.

On walks Labradors have a natural instinct to find things and deliver them safely to their owners. They may even pick up dead squirrels, rabbits or dried cowpats and will present these to their owners with supreme satisfaction. These dogs are often used to retrieve more than balls and toys. On numerous occasions they have been successful in helping find missing persons. The intelligent and alert dispositions of male Labradors like Snowbell make them perfect animal helpers to humans as well as making them great search and rescue dogs deployed during national and local disasters. Labradors are also often trained to track criminals for the police. All of these retrievers frequently interact with the public. Some of them are true animal heroes saving countless lives every year. In short they are born to retrieve, it's what they do best; this is their very life mission.

The Lord Jesus Christ came into this world to rescue and retrieve both the spiritually dead and wounded with the purpose of bringing them back to a loving Father who is waiting for them. In the gospels we are told "For the Son of Man is come to seek and to save that which is lost". (Luke 19:10). Our God is a restoring God. His purpose is to give us life here on earth and life eternal with Him in heaven. The thief—which is the devil—comes only to steal, kill and to destroy, but Jesus said "I am come that they might have life and that they might have it more abundantly" (John 10:10). Christ's very own mission statement at His miraculous birth, during His youth and when He died and rose again at Calvary, has always read as one who rescues and restores the lost. When His parents failed to understand

Him as a child He told them: "How is it that you sought me, did you not know that I must be about my Father's business" (Luke 2:49). The Father's business is the business of restoring the lost. It's the business of taking that which is spiritually dead and wounded in order to ensure that no one is lost. Christ said in the book of John "Of them that thou gavest me I have lost none" (John 18:9).

I became disturbed after reading a horrific tale of a little dog that was chained up for ten years. The dog had no blanket, no toy, not even a bone. Often it had no water or clean water, until mercifully it was rescued. According to the Animal Advocates Society website, this dog was found at night, lying in the frozen mud, with the snow falling and lying in her own excrement. Despite several attempts by neighbours to have her rescued she remained neglected. She was dehydrated and barely able to walk because of painful hips and her coat was weighed down by clumps of caked mud. Neighbours testified that her owners were seen urinating on her and even named her Judas. Thanks to the efforts of the AAS, (Animal Advocates Society) a home was found for this little dog. Two very special people loved her dearly and made her a member of their family. This family nursed her back to health with love and kindness and when she eventually died she took with her all of the memories of love, warmth and good food and even fun.

How similar it is in the life of every restored and redeemed believer. Prior to their salvation experience, many were chained up, left to perish in their sins, unwanted and disliked by the world until Christ came and saved them through His great mercy. He made them members of the family of God and has protected them ever since. Just as Snowbell would go to any lengths to retrieve a ball, a stick, or a dead or wounded animal, in the very same way Jesus goes after the lost of this world. Christ is interested in the individual, something He illustrated when telling the parable of the lost sheep. He said "What man of you, having an hundred sheep, if he loses one of them, doth not leave the ninety and nine in the wilderness and go after that which is lost, until he find it"? (Luke 15:4). And again in the book of Luke Christ tells the touching story of the parable of the lost son. When his brother became angry because of all the attention the prodigal son received after being found, the father said to him "Son, you are always with me and all that I have is yours. It was right that we should make merry and be glad, for your brother was dead and is alive again, and was lost and is found" (Luke 15:31). This sort of desire to see men and women rescued and restored prompts the question—do Christians have this same heart that Jesus has? Do they go out into the highways and byways in order to find the dead and the wounded within their own society? Do they even understand the central message of the gospel which is to recover and restore?

In our world there are many broken people. The retrieving instinct has never been more required within the church of Jesus Christ than it is today and there are many ways to retrieve. Not everyone should be dressed with a sign that says "Ye must be born again" or carry a bag of gospel tracts in their pocket ready for delivery to every person they meet. Certainly there are some people who are born for this style of ministry and most compatible with door to door outreach or street evangelism, yet not everyone is cut out for this kind of outreach. We all have varying gifts and talents and it's in the area of our competence and excellence that God wants us to shine. If you are uncomfortable in a certain ministry that's a sure sign you're not meant to be there. God doesn't want us operating out of our comfort zone. As much I would like, I cannot sing solo on a Sunday evening at our church. Yet I can write, present and broadcast and even preach. I know my own gifts given by Almighty God, but I have also worked out my limitations. The apostle Paul says in the book of Ephesians, "And he gave some, apostles and some, prophets and some, evangelists and some pastors and teachers; for the perfecting of the saints, for the work of the ministry, for the edifying of the body of Christ; till we all come in the unity of the faith and of the knowledge of the Son of God unto a perfect man, unto the measure of the stature of the fullness of Christ" (Ephesians 4:11-13). A unified church going out to reach the lost and working at full capacity will be so much more effective compared to a church in disunity that doesn't know its correct function. I once entitled a sermon I brought in Romania—"stop preaching, if you're not reaching!" It's the willingness to reach which births the ability to change and we can all become reachers in some form or another.

When I reflect upon the hopelessness of the lives of many of the children in Romania before they were rescued by Christ and given shelter and solace in the Children's House, I could literally weep. Some didn't even have shoes on their feet and life was tough to say the least. One young girl arrived with just a little bag—it was all she had in the world. When she went to bed at night she took the bag with her and clasped it tightly until daybreak. On occasions when Mama Louise would creep into her room and gently attempt to remove the bag from her, amazingly she would wake in time to keep it beside her. It may have been worthless and there was nothing in it, yet it was all she had and she wasn't about to lose it to anyone. She not only needed Jesus, she needed us to help her up and on her way. Many of these children were orphans with no real hope in the world until we entered their lives and Jesus restored them.

People are strung out today on drink and drugs, many are devoid of direction and without help they end up lost and confused, but there is hope when Jesus finds them. Christ's own retrieving attributes are clear through the words of 1 Timothy 1:15 which states "This is a faithful saying and worthy of all acceptation that Christ Jesus came into the world to save sinners". Notice Paul specifies just who Jesus has come to rescue—sinners. His work at the cross when He shed His blood was accomplished for sinners everywhere. In the book of Matthew we read how Jesus enlightened both the scribes and Pharisees about his mission in life with the words "It is not the healthy who need a doctor, but those which are sick" (Matthew 9:12). Christ refused to withdraw from sinful men such as the Pharisees even when they were offended. The great Bible commentator Matthew Henry wrote: "If the world had been righteous there had been no occasion for Christ's coming, either to preach repentance or to pay for our forgiveness". Imagine the King of Kings and Lord of Lords coming all the way to this sinful world just for the purpose of saving lost sinners. Yet that's what He's been doing for centuries. The Lord Jesus has picked up many who have lost their way. A restoring Saviour, He has redeemed them forevermore. As Jude records: "Now unto Him who is able to keep you from falling and present you faultless before the presence of His glory with exceeding joy" (Jude 1:24). To retrieve is ultimately to protect.

Brutis was a seven-year-old Golden Retriever in 2004 when he suddenly became a hero. The loveable pooch snatched up a coral snake as it was slithering dangerously close to a young child, suffering a near deadly bite from the snake in the process. His heroics didn't go unnoticed, however, as Brutis was promptly flown to Los Angeles to receive the National Hero Dog Award. Likewise Hurricane Katrina was a miserable occurrence for everyone in the southern part of the US, but inspiring stories of heroism have helped give victims something to smile about. That's certainly the case with Katrina; the ironically named black Labrador who saved a drowning man before rising flood waters claimed his life. The dog was later rescued by rescue teams and honoured with a standing ovation at the Genesis Awards. Why does this breed of dog risk their own lives to save others? Because to protect and restore is part of their retrieving instinct. Restoration is also a pivotal part of the Christian life. God not only saves, He keeps and restores, even the years that have been wasted and lost.

The New Testament story in the book of Luke, involving Jesus and two of his disciples, James and John, tells how Christ was rejected by the Samaritans, provoking James and John to want to call down fire from heaven and consume them like Elijah once did in the Old Testament. But Jesus turned and rebuked his two disciples, saying, "You know not what manner of spirit you are of, for the Son of Man is not come to destroy men's lives, but to save them" (Luke 9:55).

People are turned away from the gospel not solely due to the distractions of this world, but equally by a wrong presentation of the gospel of peace. Our understanding of God will ultimately define our message to men. The over-emphasis upon the legalism of the Old Testament in preference to the lovely message of grace in the New Testament often drives potential converts away from God's House. Much of this kind of ministry is preached only to control converts and keep them in fear. Truth is important, yet possessing grace is imperative in the life of every Christian, for our Lord Jesus Christ is full of grace. The Bible reminds us that the "letter", a reference to Old Testament law, kills, but it is the "spirit", a reference to New Testament grace, which brings forth life. Man can be harsh in his judgement—as is illustrated by the ruthless and callous approach of both James and John who, let's not forget, were two of the chosen twelve apostles. Their motive may have been admirable to display loyalty to their King, but their methods fell far short of the standards Christ requires from His followers. They wanted to kill and write off the Samaritans, probably due to prejudice and other long-standing sores, but Christ showed them just why He came to this world in the first place: to show His great love, forgiveness and restorative power. John puts it like this: "For God sent not his son into the world to condemn the world, but that the world through him might be

71

saved" (John 3:17). Many servants of God misunderstand what loyalty to Christ is actually all about. True loyalty is to manifest the same love, grace and goodness that are found in Christ. In short, it is possessing similar Christ-like grace and love in all that we do and say. There's little point in standing for truth when we fail to exhibit grace or love in our own lives. Our message to men reveals our own understanding of God.

It's enlightening to read how many years later when John was an older man he began to express this great love through the words of scripture. Age has a way of mellowing all of us and this was John's experience. He went from having the desire to call down fire from heaven to demonstrating God's true nature and God's love. In 1 John he stated, "Beloved let us love one another for God is love and everyone that has love is born of God and knows God. He that loves not knows not God for God is love. In this was manifested the love of God towards us because that God sent His only begotten Son into the world that we might live through him. Herein is love, not that we loved God, but that He loved us and sent His Son to be the propitiation for our sins. Beloved, if God so loved us, we also ought to love one another" (1 John 4:7-11). With God, through Christ, there is mercy to pardon the greatest sins and grace to change the greatest sinners and make them holy. Mike Murdock writes "Anything broken can be repaired. Anything closed can be open. Anything lost can be recovered".

The hymn writer, Francis H. Rowley, penned "I was lost, but Jesus found me, found the sheep that went astray, threw His loving arms around me, and drew me back into the way". During the chaos of the 9/11 attacks when almost 3,000 people died, nearly 100 search and rescue dogs and their owners scoured Ground Zero for survivors. Almost a decade later 12 of those canine survivors were commemorated in a touching series of portraits titled 'Retrieved'. The dogs worked tirelessly to search for anyone trapped alive in the rubble along with countless emergency services workers and members of the public. Most of those search and rescue dogs were Labradors or Golden Retrievers.

The lovely Saviour of the world is full of gifts to heal, guide and encourage, yet His greatest function is to find the lost and restore their lives. He was born to retrieve. "To this end was I born, and for this cause came I into the world that I should bear witness unto the truth. Everyone that is of the truth hears my voice" (John chapter 18:37).

Jesus Christ has Himself undertaken the biggest search and rescue mission in history, larger than 9/11 and many other high profile cases of missing persons—and it's a search that won't end until all of His children have been found.

CHAPTER TEN

TIME FOR A GOOD WASH

"Purge me with hyssop and I shall be clean, wash me and I
shall be whiter than the snow". (Psalm51).

LESSON 10—THERE'S ONLY ONE
WAY TO TRULY FEEL CLEAN.

Labradors are renowned for their love of the outdoors; not good
news if you happen to own one, of course. These dogs are not
only capable of walking the legs off their master; they also end
up incredibly dirty following any form of recreation. This situation was
often compounded in Snowbell's case because when he was young he was
a cuddly white Labrador and any mud and dirt became all too visible on
his normally bright white coat. He would always start out in the morning
clean as a whistle, but as the day progressed he became muddier and
muddier until eventually his coat became entirely black.

One day after my car had driven in through the gates, he managed to
sneak down the lane for some "unauthorised" play-time, only to return
completely covered in mud and dirt. For whatever reason he then decided
it would be a good idea to jump all over me and shake off all the dirt on
to my new suit. I'd left the front door of my car wide open while I went to
look for him enabling him to also jump into the front seats and leave his
dirty paw prints everywhere. If I could have caught up with him afterwards

I would have given him a great slap, but before I could reach the car he sprinted out and down the yard into his hut.

As a rule, dogs don't necessarily require frequent baths, but they can benefit from a periodic shampoo, using a specially formulated dog shampoo with a conditioner included. In Snowbell's case, periodic was getting to be every other day!!! We just couldn't seem to keep him clean and we liked him clean. The whiter he was kept, the more appealing he was.

I still remember with affection Snowbell's first ever bath. It was a comical experience and didn't go very well. We had to chase him up and down, he was panting, drooling, whining, and at the end we were left with a not so clean dog and we seemed to be wetter than he was. He clearly appeared very unsure about his first ever bath, even scared, yet it eventually became something he would so look forward to. It's no secret that many dogs dread bath time but, as time progressed, Snowbell didn't dread it at all; instead he seemed to thoroughly enjoy it.

That first time, however, I had to almost force him into the bath which left him feeling quite nervous. Once he got used to it he revelled in his new activity. Whether it was the removal of all of the dirt that relieved him, or the immense stroking and patting during the drying off period which gave him the most satisfaction, I'm still not sure. Nevertheless, jumping into his little bath and freshening up undoubtedly became one of his favourite pastimes. The more water that was poured over him, the happier he seemed to be and he certainly knew how to drench everyone else around him. Franklin P. Jones observes: "Anyone who doesn't know what soap tastes like, never washed a dog". The splashing of water was something to behold and the more excited he became the bigger the splashes became.

Once he settled down, however, it was as though he'd gone to the local massage parlour for a full body rub. Sometimes he would sit on the edge of his bath sunbathing, then slowly roll back in and cool off. What a character! I once put a hat on him and he looked like a sun worshipper living it up in Spain or costa-del somewhere! After his great wash his eyes and ears, nose and coat would all be shining again just like that first day he entered our home from the dog shop. When he emerged from his little tub, wagging his tail and shaking his coat, he was literally white as snow, not to mention lapping up all the attention he received from his many admirers. He had a new spring in his step and additional confidence. He was quite a poser, you know! "Look at me!" he would indicate. "Am I beautiful or what?" was his message as he strutted around the grounds as if he owned the place. Unquestionably he was a beautiful dog and post-bath he was so bright and white it made even a previous self-confessed dog-hater like me proud to say he was ours. A dog that's clean and odour-free is a joy to be around. Let's be honest, there's nothing pleasant about being able to smell a dog when you enter the front door of a house, or to witness your dog up to his eyes in mud. But to observe him running around clean as a whistle is a beautiful feeling for any dog owner, particularly when he wags his tail and sports his bright new coat.

When I would see him as black as one's boot, then witness his transformation into a gleaming, radiant-looking dog following his regular wash. It reminded me of someone else who removes all of our own stains and washes whiter than the snow—the Saviour of the world the Lord Jesus Christ. God's own remedy for sin, Jesus Christ, is the only one capable of washing us from head to toe and thus giving us a clean bill of health. The book of 1st John tells us that "The blood of Jesus Christ, God's Son, cleanses us from all sin," while the book of Hebrews records that: "Without the shedding of Christ's blood there is no remission of sins" (Hebrews 9:22). There's only one way to feel truly clean and that is through the blood of Jesus.

Many of us start out in life with great dreams and the best of intentions, blissfully unaware that we need to be washed or cleansed at all, yet this sinful and corrupt world has a way of diminishing those same dreams and intentions. Before long we become soiled by the fallen age in which we live and our own coats, so to speak, become foul and unfit for use. Sin makes us feel dirty, the wages of which are death, according to the apostle Paul. Few truly enjoy living in sin, even though much is made of this so-called enjoyment. One of the great Bible commentators, Matthew Henry, once wrote, "sin is a brat that no-one wants to own", a reference to the consequences attached to sinful habits.

It's known that grooming is an important part of a dog's care. It not only makes the dog look better, but contributes to the dog's physiological and psychological health. This is particularly evident when animal rescue shelters advertise pictures of dogs which have been mistreated or neglected. Their little faces are sad and helpless and their general condition is usually extremely poor. They are thin and straggly and their coats are often filthy and tattered looking. You can tell that they are depressed, unhappy and forlorn. Similarly the mood of mankind becomes depraved and more depressed at the state of his uncleanliness. We may think we are enjoying ourselves in our own sin, but eventually the consequences catch up with us.

King David was a man who understood something of the pain of an unclean and sinful life. After he had committed murder and adultery David cried unto God in Psalm 51 with the words: "Purge me with hyssop and I shall be clean, wash me and I shall be whiter than the snow". To purge means to purify, or to remove that which is unwanted, that which produces guilt. Our conscience is purified by the blood of Jesus. In the same way, David knew that there was only one remedy for his sinful life and sinful heart and that was God's forgiveness and daily cleansing. In another portion of that great confession, David says: "Create in me a clean heart O God and renew within me a right spirit". He also cries: "Have mercy upon me, oh God, according to your loving kindness, according unto the multitude of your tender mercies, blot out my transgressions".

Such forgiveness and cleansing has been made available today due to the provision of the Lord Jesus Christ, who shed his own blood upon the cross at Calvary that men and women might be saved and set free from their sins. It's sad when we take a "do-it-yourself" approach to sin and try to clean ourselves. This just isn't effective. Only the blood of Jesus can suffice.

Commercial cleaning companies spend millions advertising their products as the best around. Washing powders, bathroom cleaning materials and equipment to remove dirt and grime from kitchen sinks and ovens are all heavily marketed as well as the cure for stained clothes and grubby homes. Yet what can wash away the sins of men? The Bible says only the blood of Jesus can leave us looking whiter than white. Christ's blood doesn't only wash the worst of our sins, or even the most of them, but the Bible promises us that Christ removes all of our sins.

J. Pierpont Morgan was a noted American financier and multimillionaire of an earlier generation. Before his death he composed a will consisting of 37 articles and 10,000 words. While Mr. Morgan had been involved in transactions involving millions of dollars during his lifetime, he left no doubt as to what was the most important transaction he ever made. In his will he wrote the following: "I commit my soul in the hands of my Saviour, full of confidence that having redeemed me and washed me with His most precious blood, He will present me faultless before the throne of my heavenly Father. I entreat my children to maintain and defend, at all hazards and at any cost of personal sacrifice, the blessed doctrine of complete atonement of sins through the blood of Jesus Christ once offered and through that alone". J. Pierpont Morgan recognised the priceless value of the blood of Christ with regard to the believer. This man could afford to buy almost anything he wanted, but not the blood of Jesus. Instead Christ's blood had purchased him. As Paul writes in the first book of Corinthians "Ye are not your own. For you are bought with a price: therefore glorify God in your body, and in your spirit, which are God's" (1 Cor. 6:19-20). The apostle Peter reminds us that we were: "not redeemed by corruptible things, such as silver and gold, but with the precious blood of Christ, as of a lamb without blemish and without spot" (1 Peter 1:9). The coats of millions have been transformed from black to white due to the regeneration process provided by Almighty God. The good news is that our hearts and lives, which were ruined by riotous living and by the sinfulness of our generation, can be restored by a merciful and loving God. It doesn't matter what your past has been Christ can cleanse you of every sin. "And such were some of you, but you are washed, you are sanctified, but you are justified in the name of our Lord Jesus Christ and in the Spirit of our God" (1 Corinthians 6:11). The apostle Paul explains it like this "For we ourselves also were sometimes foolish, disobedient, deceived, serving lusts and pleasures, living in malice and envy, hateful and hating one another. But after that, the love of God our Saviour toward man appeared, not by works of righteousness which we have done, but according to the washing of regeneration and renewing of the Holy Ghost, which He shed on us abundantly through Jesus Christ our Saviour" (Titus 3:3-8). When we are washed in the blood of Jesus, we are also sanctified. We have peace through the blood. Having been alienated from God, our peace comes through the blood of Christ's cross. It is His great love for us that has cleansed us from our sins. It is this great love that makes us righteous and right in the sight of God. John writes in the book of Revelation "Unto Him that has loved us and washed us from our sins in His own blood" (Revelation 1:5).

Many believers, despite claiming to be saved for years, continue to carry a great burden of guilt. Often this guilt is actually over past sins, proving that they have a general sense of being unworthy of the name of Jesus Christ. Now while Paul the apostle tells us that "All have sinned and fallen short of the glory of God" (Romans 3:23), he goes on to remind us that we are "justified freely by his grace through the redemption that is in Christ Jesus, whom God has sent forth to be a propitiation through faith in his blood, to declare his righteousness for the remission of sins that are past, through the forbearance of God" (Romans 3:24-25). The word propitiation simply means that which returns us to a state of favour or goodwill. In other words, when Jesus shed His blood at Calvary, He returned us to a favourable state with God. Because our past sins have been forgiven and even remitted, we are restored to a sinless state, not because we are not sinners, but because our faith in the blood of Jesus removes all past sins; thus setting us free from any guilt. If we are truly saved we will praise God daily for cleansing us in Christ's blood, which is mentioned by design in the last book of the Bible. John writes "Unto him that has loved us and washed us from our sins in his own blood and hath made us kings and priests unto God and his father; to him be glory and dominion for ever and ever. Amen" (Revelation 1:5-6).

Christ loved his creation even before it existed. The second book of Timothy records that His grace "was given us in Christ Jesus before the world began". Of course, it's one thing to say we love someone or something, but it's entirely another to demonstrate it. "Sure you know I love you" said a husband to his lonely wife, but the same man would never bring her flowers, refused to take her out for dinner, never held her hand and never made her feel special. Christ proved His love and made His creation feel special by offering Himself upon the cross to bear our sins in His own body. Here was the supreme manifestation of His love and the obvious meaning of the words "unto him that has loved us". If He loved us when we were unloving, unlovely and unlovable, what confidence we can now have that He will continue to love us as He teaches us to love Him and recreates us in the image of Himself.

I recall a sermon which I preached to my Romanian congregation one Sunday morning entitled "It's time for a good wash!" It provoked quite a reaction from the congregation and raised more than a few eyebrows. Initially the congregation assumed I was referring to their physical condition when, in fact, my subject related totally to their spiritual welfare. Many of our congregation were from the local village of Carani and many of them were extremely poor. Most of them materially speaking had very little, yet in Christ they were now rich and had found a different kind of prosperity. They had found a friend called Jesus to be with them in their darkest days and there were many dark days for the people of our church. It was hard enough not having any financial certainty, but when the floods came and the winds blew, when the snow came and the rain then refused to come due to droughts, many of these faithful people didn't even have a meal to put on the table. It would have been easy to give up; easy to become neglected and not to care. On the contrary, however, many of them found strength and hope in Christ, a hope they had never previously experienced. They found help in our church and in our staff and in their new-found faith in God. As I spoke that morning about the blood of Jesus and its power to cleanse, the sermon immediately resonated with many of these people. They stood and worshipped in a manner I had never witnessed them do so before. It was as though the Spirit of God had switched on a light and opened a window to their souls. It was an extraordinary morning in the presence of God. We finished the meeting with a wonderful hymn entitled, "Are you washed in the blood". It was a rousing service where both adults and children alike received the Saviour that memorable morning. The words go as follows and ask a great question: "Are you washed in the blood, are you washed in the soul cleansing blood of the lamb, are your garments spotless, are they white as snow, tell me, are you washed in the blood of the lamb?"

How about you? Do you feel dirty? Do you require a good wash? Do you need strength and hope when the storms of life are raging? Then why not take a bath in the blood of Jesus? He'll clean you up for sure.

CHAPTER ELEVEN

NOT JUST WASHED, BUT BAPTISED TOO

"Therefore go and teach all nations, baptizing them in the
name of the Father and of the Son and of the Holy Ghost"
(Matthew 28:19).

LESSON 11—BAPTISM IS NOT AN OPTION,
IT'S A COMMAND.

All Labradors enjoy romping through the countryside and off-lead runs are known to be essential for this energetic breed if they are not to become bored or tubby. Snowbell was no exception. The amount of exercise both he and any adult dog requires varies depending on the age, lifestyle, breeding and fitness level, but dog experts say that a rough guideline is always as much as you can both manage. Certainly Snowbell, like most Labradors, would have left you breathless and soaking. He just adored water; indeed it was a miracle if he didn't manage to get his paws wet on some stretch of walk. He would often become totally submerged before returning to the side of his walker, anxious to share the experience by shaking himself all over you. Ambrose Pierce said: "the most affectionate creature on earth is a wet dog".

I, for one, could not disagree with that for many a day I got drenched by his antics in the water. A Labrador like Snowbell has a thick windproof and waterproof coat—perfect for dips in the local river or for walks on cold, wet wintry evenings. It's why Snowbell never seemed to mind about the freezing conditions of a Romanian winter lake, but would plunge in regardless.

Historically, many Labradors, especially retrievers, spent time swimming in icy water between the fishing boats. It's even been suggested that they were used to help with the pulling in of heavy fishing nets. Their keen natural love of water, however, allows them to pick up the scent of a pond or a stream from long distances away. If given the opportunity Snowbell would frequently disappear, only to be found up to his neck in mud and dirty water, much of which ended up being deposited upon me and the front seats of my car. These dogs simply live to retrieve things from water and this is one of their favourite pastimes.

The Labrador has a tendency to leap straight into streams and canals and their owners may find themselves dragging the dog out because the bank is too steep for it to scramble out unaided. Such is their desire for water, many Labradors have been known to leap into a frozen lake in winter and fall through the ice, needing to be rescued by their owners.

While I never had that experience with Snowbell, I do fondly recall having to rescue him as a puppy from, of all places, our garden swimming pool which was built for the children. It had just been filled up one morning when Snowbell became intrigued with it. Fortunately I was watching from the upstairs apartment window when I noticed him dipping his paws into the water. It was like watching a child at the beach for the very first time. Tentatively he would put his paw towards the water, and then take it back again. I was reminded of the days when as a child I used to dip my foot in the water at Ballyholme beach in Bangor, having no intention of going in for a swim due to the freezing temperature of the water. Thankfully what was about to happen to Snowbell never actually happened to me. Suddenly he slid right over the edge of the pool and into the water and looked very much in distress. He hadn't yet become familiar with such a great amount of water and looked like he was drowning. I sprinted down stairs and, with the help of our security man, scooped him out of the water before drying him off with a hair dryer. He looked like a drowned rat and clearly wasn't amused. We all felt so sorry for him, but it wouldn't be long before Snowbell would become an avid water dog with a real passion for streams, canals and water of any sort. His early fears were soon erased as his Laboratorial instincts took over. He soon came a long way from the first time I had to insist he took his first bath and from that moment when he nearly drowned.

This desire to embrace water and become baptised is also expected from every Christian once they have accepted Jesus Christ as their personal Saviour. It's not an option, but a command. Jesus said in the book of John, "Truly I say to you, unless a man is born of water and the Spirit, he cannot enter into the Kingdom of God" (John 3:5) and again in the book of Matthew, the Lord Jesus stated "Therefore go and teach all nations, baptizing them in the name of the Father and of the Son and of the Holy Ghost" (Matthew 28:19).

Of course, not all baptisms go according to plan. Many a story has been told by a minister about baptisms which went horribly wrong, as I also found to my cost in Romania. For example, you really do need to ensure that you have someone to help pull out of the water those who are being baptised. We used to baptise the children and members of our church in the large swimming pool beside the church. The sight of sometimes 20 people standing in robes waiting to be baptised often made the neighbours curious enough to peer through the fence and see what was going on. Their curiosity was further aroused when the service ended up becoming more like an open-air gospel rally service. One night, however, when another pastor failed to make it to our service, I decided to hold the baptismal service myself. Everything was going well until someone resembling Goliath got into the pool. He was not just tall, but very heavily built and I hadn't really given enough thought as to how I would perform this particular baptism. After I pushed him under the water, naturally I couldn't get him back up again. He couldn't swim and, as he flapped fearfully in the water, we thought he was going to drown. The laughter from those watching was most embarrassing. Even the cooks were leaning out of the kitchen window and were in utter hysterics. It's a night they will never forget. Only consolation was, of course, that if anyone went through the waters of full immersion it certainly was this poor fellow. He was literally soaked, had managed to swallow half of the pool, yet was still able to raise a "Praise the Lord" at the end of it all.

What is baptism then and why be baptised at all? The word baptizo in Greek is translated "baptize" in the New Testaments, meaning to "dip" or "immerse". Baptism is an outward sign of an inner work. It's proof we have died to the flesh and become alive in the spirit. It's the evidence of spiritual rebirth by the quickening of regeneration by the Holy Ghost, having been washed in the blood of Jesus Christ. Baptism is for those who have been redeemed by the precious blood of Jesus.

The Christian Institute's article on baptism entitled: "Is Baptism by Immersion the only correct way to be baptised" is, in my opinion, a most balanced, respectful and thoughtful conclusion on the subject of water baptism. I like it because it highlights three modes (or methods) of water baptism used in Christian churches today: immersion, in which the person is completely submerged; affusion, that is pouring—and aspersion (sprinkling). While many people have been baptised by the methods of pouring and sprinkling, it seems clear that immersion is the biblical norm; nevertheless some believers clearly resist the command to be baptised in this manner. An Ethiopian eunuch once asked the apostle Phillip "See, here is water, what is hindering me from being baptised?" (Acts 8:36).

Phillip then proceeded to take him "down into the water" and baptised him there and then. This was also how John the Baptist performed the ceremony of what is termed "believer's baptism" in the river Jordan, while Jesus Himself evidently went through the process of full immersion. Scripture tells us: "And Jesus, when He had been baptised, went up immediately out of the water" (Matthew 3:16). Interestingly the Ethiopian eunuch went "down into the water" while Christ came "up out of the water"; the implication is that both became totally immersed—"whelmed in the river"—and that's how God expects His followers to experience their own baptism.

When I was younger, I was taken to church by my mother and was baptised as a child by the method of sprinkling. I loved that particular church and it's still dear to my heart today. However, it was only later when I gained a greater understanding of the subject of baptism that I became persuaded by the method of full immersion. It also seems quite apparent that the Bible teaches that baptism before belief is irrelevant, thus ruling out the practice of baptism of infants as being of any true spiritual significance.

Since they are incapable of belief, infant baptism is therefore more about parents choosing to symbolically dedicate their children to God. Is there therefore salvation without baptism? This is a question I have often heard asked. Many teach that the answer is a definite no, but if this is true then what about the story of the thief on the cross? Jesus said to a man who had repented of his sins, but hadn't time to be baptised in water, "Today you shall be with me in paradise". Without doubt the thief received the gift of salvation. There was no water baptism, but there was full immersion in Jesus Christ through belief. It's important to stress, however, that such an incident is an exception to the rule. As Christians we are commanded to be baptised. Baptism is not an option; it's a command. Evangelical Christians are divided, of course, on the question of which modes are proper forms of baptism. Common sense indicates, and, it's important to highlight, that the water is not all important and that other modes may be used in exceptional circumstances. God accepts the believer on the basis of his or her faith in Christ and the desire to obey Him, not on the basis of how much water covers the body when they were baptised. Therefore the church should gladly welcome into fellowship all those whom Christ has accepted. (Romans 15:7, 1 John 1:3).

The most renowned story in the Bible regarding baptism is discovered when Jesus sought out John the Baptist and was Himself baptised. It was an amazing encounter. At first John refused to baptise Jesus protesting that it was he who had need of baptism by Jesus, but the Lord simply replied "Allow it to be so, in order to accomplish all righteousness" (Matthew 3:15).

As a true follower of Christ, John agreed to the wishes of his Master. As true followers of Christ we also will want to please the Lord by emulating Him through baptism with water unless, of course, circumstances beyond our control prevent it, such as ill health or disability, although even this fails to deter some people. Remarkably I have witnessed disabled people in our own church being lifted out of wheel chairs in order to go through the waters of baptism. While not every disabled person can accomplish this, nevertheless watching those who can put their faith in action is always such an inspirational encounter. I know of others who have a genuine fear of water and this is actually quite common amongst people who never learned to swim. But many of these people have still trusted Christ and gone through the process of water baptism by full immersion. Our Lord and Saviour set the example and established water baptism as an ordinance of His church. He went through the process of full immersion to symbolise His own death, burial and resurrection at Calvary. The illustration was death to self, burial with Christ and resurrection with Christ to be with the Father.

Baptism by water is therefore clearly established in the Bible, so like the golden retriever Labrador, we should totally submerge ourselves enthusiastically into the waters before returning to our master to dry off and walk in the newness of life. This ought to be a thoroughly enjoyable and fulfilling experience for every Christian.

I have always felt a superior level of anointing and greater strength following my own baptism years ago and I know others have had such an experience. A supernatural power becomes available to us that just wasn't there prior to our baptismal experience. As Paul wrote in the book of Romans: "Therefore we are buried with him by baptism into death that like as Christ was raised up from the dead by the glory of the Father even so we also should walk in the newness of life". (Romans 6:4).

There can be no clearer picture of how Christ intended us to be baptised than to think of a Labrador like Snowbell running head first with such joy into the water, then shaking off the water and running into the delighted arms of his master. Baptism is not an option; it's a command. Have you been baptised yet?

Chapter Twelve

Returning To Give Thanks

"Giving thanks always, for all things unto God, even the
Father, in the name of the Lord Jesus Christ"
(Ephesians 5:20).

Lesson 12—Thankfulness is a godly quality.

I t's one of the most endearing, yet least visible traits left in the world today—the desire to give thanks. Appreciation may be rare but when it's sincerely expressed, there's a feel-good factor for all involved. Thankfulness is magnetic.

I'd been working in Romania for some years and I was giving of myself on a daily basis due to the incredible need all around me. Sadly many responded as if it was their right to receive. Thanksgiving was occasionally in evidence, but not very often. Then one day, when I least expected it, my heart was truly touched when someone finally came back to genuinely give thanks. It wasn't a local whom we had helped out of trouble, nor was it one of the children, as many of these were living in a palace compared with where they had come from. Instead it was my little dog Snowbell.

Having just received his daily offering of food which, as usual, he rushed to place in his makeshift kitchen, this wonderful growing Labrador literally charged round the corner at break-neck speed and jumped all over me. I was now in full embrace with a dog; yes . . . . a dog! He jumped into my arms like there was no tomorrow, then retreated round the corner again no doubt to devour his neatly laid out dinner. The gesture left me speechless. Remember, I had never previously owned a dog and was quite unaware of just how amazing these animals really are. "He has just returned to give thanks", I exclaimed to my wife, who was equally taken aback at Snowbell's gratitude.

It's a moment that will be forever etched upon both of our memories. Actually the incident set a precedent. Thereafter Snowbell would regularly come back and give thanks for anything I brought him; nevertheless that first encounter is the one I will always cherish, a moment which is still precious to me. I still recall, too, how he would give me a couple of delightful little licks on my hand, arm or leg before scampering back to his food. It was as if he was saying "thank you daddy" before going on his merry way.

Does a dog really have the capacity to convey the words "thank you?" While they may not know the meaning of thank you, I'm convinced they certainly know how to express their appreciation.

They say people don't always hear what you say, but afterwards they never forget how you made them feel. Snowbell made me feel loved and appreciated and it had been a long time since I'd felt like that. Dogs are not our whole lives, of course, but they can make our lives whole due to the gratitude they show. "We shouldn't need to be thanked for our good deeds," some people maintain. They even add that God doesn't want to be thanked for anything we have received from Him. How wrong this is, especially in the light of God's Word. The need for human appreciation has never been greater, while the scriptures make clear how even Jesus desired to be thanked for his good works.

In one of the most powerful accounts of the New Testament, Jesus heals no fewer than ten people of the wretched disease of leprosy. In Bible days leprosy was a dreadful and unclean illness, contagious and contaminating in every way. It was feared by people everywhere and the most hurtful thing for those unfortunate enough to suffer from it was the fact that no-one was allowed to come anywhere close to them in case it spread further.

There were caves in a place known as the "valley of the lepers" where only those diagnosed with the disease lived. Food had to be dropped down to them on baskets and their entire contact with the outside world was cut off. It would be almost impossible to describe their condition. They had swellings and lumps over their bodies with some parts lacking any feeling. Their skin was covered in ulcers. For some there was great pain involved in the nose and throat, for others hands and feet were eaten away. Having leprosy was akin to living in hell itself. Nevertheless one day Jesus not only intermingled with and touched such people, He literally healed ten of these poor souls and set them free. Can you even begin to imagine how they must have felt? They were now clean again. They could re-enter society and live a normal life. No more isolation or rejection. They were restored and rejuvenated. Surely all ten would be bowed at the feet of Jesus in outright appreciation for what He had just accomplished for them, right? Wrong! On the contrary, just one of the ten (10%) returned to give thanks, prompting Jesus to ask the question "Were there not ten cleansed? But where are the nine? Why has only one come back to give thanks?" (Luke 17:17-18).

Christ's reaction is a very interesting one, indeed. It shows firstly that thanking God and those who have been kind to us is always the right thing to do; in our modern world it's simply referred to as having manners. I can still hear the voice of my mother ringing in my ears when I was growing up, "Say please, say thank you, say excuse me, say sorry", and today I'm so glad I had such a mother. There is nothing worse than witnessing ungrateful people devoid of manners. To give thanks with a grateful heart is what God wants from us and if we fail to give thanks we are usually the ones to suffer most. Ungrateful people are always unhappy people and their blessings can so easily be removed. The quickest cure for ingratitude is when we begin to suffer loss. Clearly we are to thank one another and God for kind and considerate gestures, for the story of the ten lepers illustrates just how much God enjoys being thanked for his goodness towards us each day.

As one who visits the homes of sick people, it amazes me how many get healed by the power of prayer, then never return to church to give thanks to the God who healed them. They go on with their lives as though nothing had happened in exactly the same way the nine lepers refused to acknowledge what Jesus had done for them. If a dog like Snowbell can return each day and express his appreciation for what he received, how much more should we return each day to thank God and each other for our own daily blessings. It's amazing how few times the gospel writers show people thanking Jesus for the miracles He worked on their behalf. There are no recorded thanks for turning water into wine. No thanks for the feeding of the five thousand. There are no thanks for the calming of the storm when the apostles' lives were in great danger. And aside from the leper who came back to give thanks, there's no evidence of anyone thanking Jesus for His miracles of healing. People do go to church, but for various reasons and not always to thank God; others go because they are forced to be there by an overzealous and concerned parent or demanding spouse.

I recall reading a story about a family who attended church which illustrates this point well. A postcard was published featuring a pilgrim family walking to church with their faithful dog to give thanks during thanksgiving season. When a mother used the picture to convince her own kids how much the children in the photograph enjoyed returning to church to give thanks her youngest wasn't so easily fooled. Instead he asked "Mum, if those kids enjoy going to church so much why is their father walking behind them with a rifle in his hand?"

Are we thankful for the church we attend without being coerced to go there and give thanks? Do we appreciate the pastor and his team? The Bible says "Rejoice always, pray without ceasing, in everything give thanks, for this is the will of God for you in Christ Jesus" (Thessalonians 5:16-18). Or as the Amplified Bible puts it "Thank (God) in everything, (no matter what the circumstances may be, be thankful and give thanks) for this is the will of God for you (who are) in Christ Jesus".

This verse is hard for many Christians to comprehend. For example, Is Paul really advocating we give thanks even for the horrible and malicious circumstances that befall us in this life? Not at all. We are not told in the Bible to give thanks for tragedies or terrible events. So how then can we give thanks in everything, regardless of circumstances? We give thanks understanding God's sovereignty and that where He does not rule, He overrules. We can therefore give thanks "in" all things, not necessarily "for" all things. Paul also comforts the child of God with the words "For we know, that all things work together for good for those who love God and those who are the called according to His purpose" (Romans 8:28). It is important to have a thankful attitude all of the time because Adam and Eve's first sin can be traced back to ingratitude. The book of Romans reminds us "For although they knew God, they neither glorified him as God, nor gave thanks to him, but their thinking became futile and their foolish hearts were darkened" (Romans 1:21). In our world, if we complain people sit up and take notice and we tend to get further in life, yet with God progress is made not by complaining, but by displaying a grateful heart and giving thanks always. Apart from the word love, the word thanks is a most powerful word indeed. Rudyard Kipling, the famous British poet, was well aware of this. The wealthy poet was said to make around one hundred dollars per word. One day after a newspaper reporter gave him a one hundred dollar bill and asked for one of his words; Kipling put the money in his pocket and said "thanks".

Try to estimate the value of God's promise of salvation, healing, mercy, provision and peace of mind and suddenly the word thanks is not just a hundred dollar word, but more like a billion dollar word. We don't, of course, necessarily have to go to church to give thanks to God. A simple prayer of gratitude is sometimes all God requires. Psalm 107 exhorts us to "Give thanks to the Lord, for He is good; His love endures forever". Similarly, Psalm 100 recommends that we: "enter God's gates with thanksgiving and His courts with praise".

In Romania we would constantly remind our children how blessed and chosen they were. While other children were running about the streets with no shoes on their feet and with no idea as to where their next meal was coming from, our children had been given all of these things by the grace of Almighty God. The following story is a case in point. As we entered a house on our visitations, the sight that greeted us was quite shocking. A lady bereft, along with her children, seated at an empty kitchen table. No plates piled with food, no glasses filled with drinks. No knives, no forks, no spoons or anything else that resembled a normal meal time; just a bare table and all of them with their heads bowed. They were praying God would send someone to help them having not eaten for days. The children were between about 3 and 13 years old. The little ones were particularly beautiful, swarthy skins and gorgeous features, but hopelessness still decorated their faces. The sadness in the eyes of the mother and her kids still grips me to this day. It was a slum area where each home regularly housed up to 10 people. Disease was rife there. The sight we were met with was horrifying and the smell of the place even worse. Things I took for granted like food, water and cleanliness were non-existent. Bad enough living in poor conditions, but starving at the same time must have felt like living in hell itself. God undoubtedly prompted both me and my translator to visit this home. The door had been left open and we could hear the voices of the children praying inside. As we walked into the small living room we immediately became aware of the extent of their problem. It brought tears to our eyes, yet I'm so glad we stumbled upon this famished family. Thereafter we were regularly able to help them, although our contribution to them and others was just a drop in the ocean compared with the massive need all around us. Often I visited people in Romania who couldn't afford to pay for dental treatment and were in such pain with toothache, they had to pull their own teeth out. Meanwhile, our children had their personal dentist, provision, protection and potential in life, unlike scores of other children left bereft of these same things. Many of these impoverished Romanian children lived down in the sewers in order to try and keep warm in wintertime. Can you imagine that? The smell and the uncomfortable nature of such a life would have been unthinkable for most of us, yet this was life to many children in those days in Romania. Temperatures in winter could be as low as—22 degrees Celsius, while in summer they had to endure soaring temperatures of up to 44 degrees Celsius. Many of the children froze to death in the winter and died from heat exhaustion in the summer. Others died after being attacked by older, more violent children, some of whom carried knives not just for protection, but also as a means of keeping control of what they viewed as their personal territory. Mercifully there were some wonderful people with a gift to work with street children who constantly ministered to such kids, but the truth is many of them were beyond reach having sadly acclimatised to such an adverse lifestyle. No wonder we constantly encouraged our kids to "give thanks" and "taste and see that the Lord is good".

We must constantly thank God for His goodness which, of course comes in so many forms. First and foremost we must always thank Him for His presence, for without the presence of God in our lives we would be most miserable and dependent upon ourselves, yet the Lord has never forsaken us. People may have deserted us when we needed them many times, but the Lord has been with us at all times and in all situations. His presence has given us peace and rest. His presence in our lives makes the difference in every situation we face. His presence brings us great joy. The Bible tells us "In thy presence is fullness of joy and at thy right hand are pleasures forever more" (Psalm 116:11). What's wonderful about the presence of God is how it operates not just when things are going well in our lives, but also when life is full of obstacles, hindrances and even persecutions. God's presence settles us and gives peace to prevail when ordinarily we would not have been able to cope.

We must thank God too for His amazing protection because we are not destroyed because of His mercies and His grace. There are so many dangers and hidden snares in this world and yet God has protected us so far. I lost count of the many times God protected us in Romania, probably also in ways we were not even aware of. I have lost count of the many times when others have buckled due to the pressures of life, yet God has protected his children and kept them safe from harm. "A thousand shall fall at thy side and ten thousand at thy right hand, but it shall not come near thee" (Psalm 91:7). How true the words: "God is our refuge and strength a very present help in time of trouble" (Psalm 46:1).

Then there is God's remarkable provision and if ever we see this provision it's in the generation we live in. Even in times of great recession God provides for His children. He is our Jehovah Jireh (my provider). The meaning of this name of God is simply "the Lord Who sees", or, "the Lord Who sees to it". To try and live without God in today's uncertain economic climate is impossible. To "go it alone" and do without this great provision for our lives is to miss out on His great blessing of provision. Due to the full blown recession we are experiencing today many people are struggling both financially and physically. It has become virtually impossible to ignore bad news about the economy. Every day people are bombarded by reports of slumping stock markets, massive layoffs and business dismissal proposals. This constant onslaught of economic gloom has hit people hard in their pockets. Social workers and other professionals around the country report that the recession has put enormous strain on many of their clients and for many this sort of stress is too much to handle. Many are falling victim to anxiety and depression and are trying to ease their fears with alcohol and other drugs. Anecdotal evidence suggests that the recession is a top reason why people are seeking mental health services. As nations continue to plunge into economic uncertainty, and millions exists below the poverty line and become more and more vulnerable, without God the future looks bleak. People need help to get a job, locate housing, access health care and provide for their children. Notwithstanding, the Christian is constantly provided for by his or her Creator God. God sees to our needs and meets them fully. He doesn't see to our greed; rather to our need. Hence the book of Psalms encourages us to "Praise the Lord with all of our soul and forget not all His benefits" (Psalm 103:2). What a mighty and compassionate God we serve!

In the story of the lepers who were healed, they forgot to thank God for his benefits, goodness and mercy. We never learned what happened to the nine that went away, nor do we really know why they failed to return to give thanks, other than the fact that they were simply ungrateful. What we do know for sure is what happened to the single one who did return. The Bible says he was made totally whole. Not only was he healed, he was made whole also. He received a full miracle in response to the simple act of thankfulness. Why are some people more thankful than others? Paul warned that in the last days gratitude would be in short supply. "But know this, in the last days perilous times will come, for men shall be lovers of themselves, lovers of money, boastful, arrogant, revellers, disobedient to parents, ungrateful, unholy, unloving, irreconcilable, malicious gossips, without self-control, brutal haters of good, treacherous, reckless, conceited, lovers of pleasure rather than lovers of God, having a form of godliness, but denying the power thereof" (2 Timothy 3:1-5). A "thanks giver" will stand out in such a world! "Giving thanks always, for all things unto God, even the Father, in the name of the Lord Jesus Christ" (Ephesians 5:20).

Let us be grateful and express our thanks to God and to one another. After all, if a dog like Snowbell can do it, surely we as humans can do it too! This day is God's gift to you, your life is a gift from God, so why not give thanks and be joyful always. Thankfulness is a godly quality.

CHAPTER THIRTEEN

DINNER TIME WAS HIS FAVOURITE TIME

So then Faith comes by hearing and hearing by the word of
God" (Romans 10:17).

LESSON 13—DEVOTIONAL TIME SHOULD BE OUR FAVOURITE TIME.

Labradors are legendary for their ability to eat anything and everything. These dogs are not just motivated by food, but live for it. Snowbell was no exception. To say he lived to eat would be something of an understatement. Primed by many thousands of years, like all dogs Snowbell was a scavenger although he, more than most, seemed to make it an art! Every day he would parade up and down at the gate waiting for my car to return from the city and there was just one thing on his mind—food! He was always, of course, glad to see me and showed his incredible affection by jumping all over me. He had another reason, however, for wanting to welcome me home: he was thinking of his greedy little belly. I don't recall him ever sharing his meal with anyone. It was his and he guarded it intensely.

In time Snowbell came to understand that his master never arrived empty-handed; there would always be sausages, chicken or even his favourite pastime—a dog bone to chew on. If I thought he couldn't count, just try putting three biscuits in my pocket and then giving him two! A hunter by trade, when he saw me returning with chicken, pork or anything else, he must have considered me to be the greatest hunter on earth. Once he'd received his daily offering, he charged around the back of the building and laid the contents out on the ground. Setting his own dinner table, he separated the food into lines before enjoying his meal. Feeding him was generally not difficult because usually he would devour anything he could get his teeth into. He was literally enjoying a dog's dinner. The phrase "a dog's dinner" is often used to imply a mess such as "dressed up like a dog's dinner" or "making" a right dog's dinner out of something. Although its origins are unknown, its most commonly believed to be linked to the fact that a dog's meal will often be full of different muddles of textures and colours and may indeed resemble a mess. Another phrase to aptly describe Snowbell's plate is "a dog's breakfast" which again is synonymous with mess or muddle. This was certainly representative of Snowbell in full dinner mode. He hardly took time to swallow and his face would be covered in food. One still had to be careful though when choosing an appropriate food for him, or the consequences could be quite grave.

Specific foods which are edible for humans and even other species of animals, can pose hazards for dogs because of their different metabolism. Some may cause only mild digestive upsets, whereas others can cause severe illness and even death. Commercial pet foods are everywhere today due to their convenience and cost, but that doesn't mean they are right for your dog. Pet food is a growth industry and large sums of money are spent on persuading the public to buy certain products via advertising, but what looks delicious on television may not be suitable for your pet. When he was a pup Snowbell became sick a number of times due to the food he was eating and after consultation with a vet I changed his diet, the result of which the sickness left him.

I noticed that if Snowbell was eating too much he was instantly susceptible to putting on weight which, of course, was bad for his health. That's why it's recommended that once the dog has been adequately fed he is later allowed out to exercise and thus work off some of that food. Of course, having a dog inspires all of us to walk more. Another consideration when feeding him was to appreciate just how much food—or rather wrong food—affected his behaviour. Dogs are like people; they have different requirements and react differently to various ingredients or elements in their diet. Some food made him hyper and almost changed his placid and gentle nature beyond all recognition. Tension levels and excitability are likely to be reduced if a dog is not forced to wait all day for food and if he is fed the right kind.

Snowbell's reaction to his food and the Christian response to the reading of the Bible, referred to as "The bread of life", are strikingly similar. Just as these Labradors live to eat, so too the man or woman who is a follower of God should possess the same desire to digest daily the Word of God. Like Snowbell, who would separate his food and organise it for consumption, the Christian is also required to separate the Word each day before applying it. Paul the Apostle wrote: "Study thyself approved unto God, a workman, not needing to be ashamed, but rightly dividing the word of truth". The Word of Truth is the daily bread in the life of every believer. According to the teachings of Jesus, it may be equally as vital as the food we consume within our physical bodies.

When asked by the devil to turn stones into bread, Jesus simply responded with the words, "Man shall not live by bread alone, but by every word that proceeds from the mouth of God" (Matthew 4:4). Physically speaking, we eat to stay alive, yet Jesus says the same is true if we are to survive spiritually in the Christian life. In the disciples' prayer Jesus taught "Give us this day our daily bread" (Matthew 6:11). And James exhorts the Christian to "receive with meekness the engrafted word, which is able to save your souls" (James 1:22). Imagine spending more time tucking into and desiring the words of scripture than we do with other things such as mobile phones, the internet, Facebook and television programmes? Surely this would enrich our lives and the church would undoubtedly be in a far stronger state than it currently enjoys. I use Facebook myself, but I'm not posting every second of the day. We must keep the balance and make time to digest good food from God's Word. David said "Thy word is a lamp unto my feet and a light unto my path"; nevertheless many Christians have, like Snowbell, consumed the wrong food and ultimately become sick. They prefer to wake up to Facebook, their iPhone and computer in preference to rising up to read God's Word. They live on CDs and DVDs and sermons from television evangelists, many of whom preach a wrong presentation of the gospel and provide them with commercial Bible teaching which tastes good, feels good, seems good, but isn't good for their bodies or souls.

Due to the generation in which we live, technology now also makes it possible for people to have church in their front living room via television and even the internet, but in many instances this has become nothing more than "easy religion". There is no effort required on behalf of the convert. This approach, of course, is acceptable if someone is ill, or in a remote spot not close to a church, but if we are in good general health and reasonably convenient to a local church, it's better to get up, drive, take the bus or a taxi or even walk to a House of God renowned for providing strong Bible teaching. To accept anything less is to compromise our relationship with God and leave us isolated from the brethren. Highlighting the dangers in following wrong teaching cannot be over-emphasised. We are living in a world full of false prophets peddling doctrinally flawed material. Other spirits are at work on a global scale due to the rise of end-times technology which appeals to the lusts of the flesh and often succeeds in luring well-meaning Christians away from the right path. Yet the solution is simple. Get back to the book—the Bible. That's where all of the answers to life are contained—within the pages of God's Word. Any book can inform you, but only the Bible can transform you! John the apostle writes "Beloved, believe not every spirit, but try the spirits whether they are of God, because many false prophets are gone out into the world" (1 John 4:1). This is God's remedy for spiritually sick Christians. No-one ever got sick through reading the pages of the Bible, but millions have been made well and restored by its healing power. The Bible says "God sent forth His word and healed them" (Psalm 104:20).

Preaching the Word of God hasn't always, of course, been tolerated, especially in Romania. Richard Wurmbrand was a Romanian Christian minister of Jewish descent and lived during the 20th century, an anti-Semitic time in Romania. Daring to suggest that Communism and Christianity were not compatible, he experienced imprisonment and torture for his beliefs. After serving 5 years of a second prison sentence, he was ransomed for 10,000 dollars. His 14-year old-son Mihai was expelled from college-level studies at three institutions because his father was a political prisoner, yet Richard Wurmbrand went on to start an underground church and showed great courage in preaching God's Word.

For centuries the Catholic Church also forbade the common people from reading the Bible in their own language, presumably because of a fear that

God's Word would speak to their hearts and liberate them from religious dogmas. Even during the early days of our own period of preaching in Romania, long after Richard Wurmbrand's experiences of persecution, regular visits were paid to our church by secret police sent to take notes on everything which was being said. Incidents like these were common and did influence some in Romania to refrain from preaching the truth. For example, on many occasions the preaching of the Word of God at our church became an offence, particularly when our church in the village of Carani began to thrive. People were leaving the surrounding Greek Orthodox churches to join us and this was proving upsetting for the authorities. Many times I recall being summoned to the local police station and Mayor's office to give an account of what I was preaching to the natives on a Sunday; a quite unnerving and intimidating experience. Remember, I was a foreigner in their country and, while I hadn't broken any laws, I was equally conscious of the fact that I had very few rights, or even friends at that stage. One day I brought a box of chocolates for the policeman in an attempt to win his favour; thankfully he loved the "orange centred ones" and decided to let me go, but it wasn't always as easy to wriggle free from such people. The wisdom of God's Word was required many times in order to stay out of trouble. Paul writes "The Word of God is quick and powerful and sharper than any two-edged sword, piercing even to the dividing asunder of soul and spirit, and of the joints and marrow, and is a discerner of the thoughts and intents of the heart" (Hebrews 4:12).

The Word of God has been described as a "Quick Word". In other words it's a living Word and this is how one becomes born again. Peter says "Being born again, not of corruptible seed, but of incorruptible, by the Word of God, which lives and abides forever" (I Peter 1:23). We serve a living God, not a dead God and His Word is living not dead. It is the inspired Word of Truth. Paul mentions that this Word is "powerful". As Luke records "For they were astonished at his doctrine, for his word was with power". (Luke 4:23). By the Word of God the worlds have been framed and are now held together. Paul says it's also a "Sharp Word", sharper than any two-edged sword. Even in this present ungodly generation the Word of God still convicts men and women of sin and of righteousness and of judgement to come. Certainly we know that God's Word is true for three significant reasons. Firstly no human would have written a standard as high as the scriptures teach. "For as the heavens are higher than the earth, so are my ways higher than your ways and my thoughts than your thoughts" (Isaiah 55:9). Secondly the changes that occur in those who embrace the Word of God are supernatural. "Therefore if any man be in Christ, he is a new creature; old things have passed away; behold all things are become new" (2 Corinthians 5:17). While thirdly, the presence of a Bible often produces a dramatic change in the atmosphere.

I still recall how this played out in remarkable fashion in our own lives in Romania just when we needed it to. A group of men had been attending our church each week, but not for spiritual reasons. They came with other intentions like reporting for the authorities and taking notes on everything and taking notes on everything I was preaching. There were at least 7 of them and I recall how they used to pull up in their cars directly outside the church just after the service had started. They were most intimidating and unfriendly individuals at first, but we ignored this and treated them as though they were genuine in their endeavours to worship with us. This continued for some weeks and became quite burdensome until one day my wife suggested that we invite the men into the home after the service for Sunday dinner to try and show them we were only in Romania to bring blessing to their country and the children of their nation. They duly accepted and were surprisingly very complimentary about the home and the food they'd received. As they were leaving, however, I gave each one of them a Romanian King James Bible which they thanked me for and guess what? We didn't see any of them ever again. What had taken place? The power of love and the Word of God had so convicted these officials they decided to leave us alone. Who knows also what God has done in their lives since, all because they received a copy of the Word of truth. A "Piercing Word", it reaches to the most innermost being and goes where no other words can go. It's a "Dividing Word", too, because many homes have been divided by it. God's Word is described as a "Discerning Word" which is why so few people really enjoy hearing it preached. People feel they are being preached at because God's Word exposes the secrets of men's hearts. They often blame the preacher, but it's the Word which has so convicted their hearts. I recollect another beautifully encouraging story in Romania which took place after I had returned from holiday. Having invited a guest speaker in my absence I asked the children and others how things went during my break. I will never forget their response. "It was good, but it wasn't you, Pastor John". Thinking they were just flattering me in order to get extra pocket money, (Oh, yes, that's true!), I then asked them to elaborate and, when I got to the bottom of their discontent, it was due to the absence of the Word of God preached in its entirety—something they had become used to in our own church.

The Bible tells us that it is 'the gospel which is the power of God unto salvation', as opposed to our own thoughts and inspirational tales. People need fed with the bread of life. In Snowbell's language, "they need steak and chips, not ice-cream and jelly". That's why many rebel and become sick, spiritually speaking. Jesus said "You shall know the truth and the truth shall set you free" (John 8:32). In Luke chapter five the people pressed in upon Jesus to hear the Word of God. How significant that these people didn't come to listen to music or be entertained, as is the case in many churches today. They worship "worship" instead of worshipping God. The Bible says the people came solely to hear the Word of Truth. It's amazing how many professing Christians claim to see visions and hear from God, yet the same people never read God's Word. God does not speak to us on advertising billboards, or by miraculous signs in the sky, or by silly visions we have dreamt up, God speaks to us by one way only—through the Word of Life. Our faith will only ever grow in proportion to how much we devour God's Word on a daily basis. "So then, faith comes by hearing and hearing by the word of God" (Romans 10:17).

I cannot prove it, of course, but it genuinely seemed to me that Snowbell's favourite meal time was on a Sunday. We called it "Chicken Dinner Day" and how he loved his Sunday lunch! He would receive the best of the leftover chicken and demolished all of it. Christians could learn from this little dog. Sunday is the Lord's Day when every church should provide its parishioners with the best of bread, a feast of God's Word. The Lord's Day should be our favourite day to receive from God the best of spiritual food. Instead, not only do many churches fail to serve up quality sermons on a Sunday, the members also fail to see the importance of being instructed on a weekly basis at the Lord's Table. Much prayer is required to change this situation.

When God wanted to feed the children of Israel in the Old Testament He sent them bread, manna from heaven. When God's servant Elijah was in want in the wilderness, the Lord instructed the ravens to bring him bread.

Jesus said "I am the bread of life, he that cometh to me shall never hunger, and he that believeth in me shall never thirst". The prophet Jeremiah wrote "Thy words were found and I did eat them and thy word was unto me the joy and rejoicing of mine heart for I am called by thy name, O Lord God of Hosts" (Jeremiah 15:16). This is what is known as "soul food". It should become part of our daily diet. Devotional time should always be our favourite time. Without it we will only starve.

CHAPTER FOURTEEN

BARKING MAD!

"The effectual fervent prayer of a righteous man availeth much".

LESSON 14—DON'T EVER BE AFRAID TO CALL UNTO GOD.

If there was one thing I didn't require during my time in Romania it was an alarm clock. Aside from the fact that just about every animal in God's creation, as well as our children, seemed to be assigned to wake me each morning, the acquisition of Snowbell to our home definitely ensured that's exactly what would happen.

The village of Carani was surrounded by all sorts of wonderful wildlife, yet none of these beautiful creatures could compare with Snowbell when it came to making an early morning racket. From dusk, this dog would place himself directly underneath our bedroom window and begin to bark and bark and bark, until finally someone had to get up and attend to him. To say he was "barking mad" was an understatement, but he knew exactly what he was doing. The phrase "barking mad" apparently emerged from the east London suburb of Barking, yet may also owe its origin to a mediaeval asylum for the insane which was at Barking Abbey. Snowbell, however, was well switched on, but he was still barking mad in another sense.

Snowbell had become used to attention from both Louise and me. Louise in particular seemed to have a full-time role spoiling him with daily massages and lots of interaction, something he now just couldn't seem to live without. Franklin P. Jones summed it up, stating "stroke a dog and you'll find a permanent job".

Of course, dogs will be dogs. They express themselves by barking for attention and also to communicate to humans. Hi there, it's me! Here I am! That seemed to be what Snowbell was saying when he barked. When a dog barks for attention it can often mean he's confused about who's in charge which wasn't surprising in our house, at least in the early days of having this pet, because we used to employ security men who would also try and master the dog each day. He was so smart his behaviour would alter depending on which security man was on duty. None of them, however, could stop his barking in the morning and no amount of encouragement by other members of staff made any difference to the situation. I just couldn't hit the snooze button on Snowbell's bladder. You can't tell your dog to clear off and make his own breakfast. You have to get up, let it out to do its business, feed it and guess what? Your own day has started earlier than you'd planned.

Snowbell would settle for a short time and then start to bark again until he always got his way. When it seemed he wasn't getting a response Snowbell would even deliberately raise the level of his barking, just in case we hadn't heard him; yet the entire neighbourhood could hear him. It's one of the reasons why on many occasions Louise or I had to scramble down the stairs to silence him. Of course, once there, he would scamper to both of us in appreciation of how we had responded to his bark. We were supposed to be controlling him, but the truth is he was now controlling us. With very little dog experience between us we probably shouldn't have allowed him to boss and master us the way that he did, but it was still so hard to resist his cries. It was genuinely hard to turn over in bed and pretend that he wasn't barking for our attention. In fact, it proved altogether impossible to ignore Snowbell's calls for friendship and fellowship. He knew we were in that bedroom and he guessed also that if he just kept barking eventually we would give in. In the end, however, it was a delight going down and reassuring him that we were still there for him and that he was much loved.

It pleased us many times, too, that Snowbell even wanted our company so much. Here was a sign of his love for us and indeed of his need of us.

I still chuckle to myself at the way in which the children would fight to take the arm of Mama Louise when they were walking outside. They used to take turns and couldn't wait to be the next in line to enjoy her company. Some would even make a scene in order to get her attention. At night we would lie in bed and hear the cry of a child downstairs and guess what? In no time Mama was there to reassure the child that all was well. This kind of behaviour and indeed Snowbell's early morning barking for attention is actually a picture of the believer's devotional and prayer-life. Just as reading God's Word is imperative in the life of a Christian, communing with God is equally vital. Snowbell's barking taught me another wonderful lesson, namely we should never be afraid to bark the odd prayer in the direction of heaven. The book of Mark says of Christ that "in the morning, rising up a great while before dawn, he went out and departed into a solitary place and there prayed" (Mark 1:35). The Lord Himself made it a daily habit to get up early in the morning and seek the Father's face for the demands of the day that lay ahead, but also just to spend time with Him. His desire was first to be with His Father before being with anyone else that He may have encountered that same day. He wanted nothing but His Father's companionship.

When we are walking with God we can never get enough of Him. We become like Daniel, whose own devotional life caused him to open his window, kneel down and pray three times daily. Daniel was caught up in a holy habit he just couldn't break. When the writing was signed and he was forbidden to pray, what did he do? Did he tell others, mourn, cry and commit suicide? No! He went into his room, knelt down and continued to pray three times a day. Despite being approximately 86 years old when this incident took place, Daniel told God in prayer about his complaint. This was his practice and he couldn't break it. If you think the account of Daniel being thrown into a den of lions for refusing to cease from prayer is nothing more than a Bible fairy story, then think again! The days of Daniel have returned and for that same reason Daniel was himself marginalised and persecuted. Some people just don't like it when we pray. They don't like it when others seek to keep God's laws even before the laws of men. They don't like it when people are faithful to God and serve Him in truth and in love. And clearly, like Daniel, they don't like it when prayer is offered first to God reverencing Him as our Creator and source of daily help. When the supervisors and governors couldn't find anything wicked about Daniel they quickly hatched a plan to try and trip him up by suggesting to the newly appointed King, following the death of Nebuchadnezzar, that no form of prayer should be offered to God for at least 30 days. The plan worked initially, but when Daniel refused to stop praying and was thrown into a den of lions, it later backfired when God shut the mouths of the lions and spared His servant Daniel—something which both pleased and angered the king who then had the supervisors and governors thrown into the same den. Daniel's reaction to the ruling that prayer was prohibited to God has much to teach our own nation at this critical time in its history. He was undoubtedly a man of courage and conviction and a man of prayer; a man who put God and His kingdom first.

Daniel's refusal to stop praying was not an insult to the government of his own generation; neither was it rebellion against authority. He had a habit he couldn't break—the habit of praying three times a day to His God; moreover, he knew that if prayer time was stopped, so too would God's blessing be hindered from the nation he lived in. The act of continued prayer therefore was more important than obeying the edict put out by Darius the King. What a lesson! The price of God's presence is time in prayer. Corrie Ten Boom said: "Don't pray when you feel like it. Make an appointment with God and keep it. A man is powerful on his knees". So often, however, we don't make this appointment or time, and we pray with the wrong motive and wonder why we end up disappointed when our prayer seemingly goes unanswered. James writes "You ask and receive not because you ask that you may consume it upon your lusts" (James 4:3). When we pray to get things it's not really prayer at all. Or, as Oswald Chambers said, "Prayer does not equip you for greater works—prayer is the greater work". Such prayer is a habit that each of us needs to form if we are to continue to walk in the Spirit and not obey the lusts of the flesh. Many have fallen not just because of a lack of reading, but due equally to lack of prayer. John Bunyan wrote "Prayer will make a man cease from sin or sin will entice a man to cease from prayer".

Early morning communion with God is essential and it's the sweetest place to begin our day which God, by His grace, has privileged us with. This prayer time and time in His presence not only cements our relationship with Him, it ensures we are led and guided by the Holy Spirit regarding major decisions which we have to take in life. I have come to learn that just one early morning hour in God's presence will expose all my best laid plans for the rest of that day, week or even month. Matthew Henry writes "It's easier to find a living man that does not breathe, than a living Christian that does not pray".

There, are, of course, different forms of prayer. There's quiet prayer accompanied by meditation such as the one Jesus experienced in the solitary place; then there's what the Bible describes as "effectual fervent prayer" which is much more demonstrative—an authentic cry from the heart for God to hear and answer the pressing problems and requests of the child of God. Just as Snowbell's barking was heard by almost the entire street and appealed for an answer, in the same way when we call upon God with great fervency we are literally crying unto God for situations in our lives. In short, God wants to show His great willingness to answer those cries and resolve our difficulties by showing His great power before men. To not pray brings misery and forfeits the blessing of God in our lives. In the words of a great hymn "What a friend we have in Jesus, all our sins and grief's to bare, all because we do not carry, everything to God in prayer".

These kinds of prayers are not usually offered every day, or even every week, but when a great need arises. No-one can pray like this every day. Our moods and situations fluctuate, yet if a need appears how good it is to know that there is One who hears and answers our calls. The Bible tells us that "The effectual fervent prayer of a righteous man availeth much". May we never feel reluctant or even frightened to cry unto God! Just as Snowbell barked continually and raised his tone when he wasn't heard, so we also when things are pressing in on us should be prepared to pray with passion. We ought to bombard heaven because God is full of compassion and delights in hearing and answering our prayers. When we engage in prayer-like warfare, it creates a miracle in our lives. Paul reminds us that "the weapons of our warfare are not carnal, but mighty through God, to the pulling down of strongholds" (2 Corinthians 10:4). Some things are only dislodged through fervent prayer. On one occasion when our backs were well and truly to the wall in Romania, I withdrew for what I thought would be a quite normal time of meditation. The children were all at school and totally unaware of the difficulties we were having in their country. It was time to pray and suddenly the Spirit of God took over and had me calling out the words, "Send the angel of God, send the angel of God". I was walking around the office repeating this sentence over and over again wondering, of course, if I had somehow lost my mind. Nevertheless, this became one of the most memorable times I've ever had in the presence of God, not because of what I prayed, but due to the results my prayer yielded afterwards. It wasn't a fantastically crafted theological prayer, on the contrary it consisted of no fewer than five words—"send the angel of God". But that's all it took for God to respond and how! Thankfully God answered that prayer in so many amazing ways thereafter. It was as though an angel or angels had indeed been dispatched from heaven to watch over us and protect us in everything we did. From that point on someone else greater and more powerful seemed to be defending us and we knew God had sent us His cavalry. Yet it took an outburst of emotion and fervent prayer before this happened. This incident with God also provoked one of my favourite sermons entitled "Don't laugh at angels". We never outgrow warfare; we must instead learn how to fight in an acceptable way to God which is to pray with great passion. Even Jesus when He was about to go to the cross prayed in such a fashion. On that most momentous day while He was with His disciples at His favourite seeking place, the Mount of Olives, the Bible says that Jesus knelt down to pray and became agonised which prompted Him to "pray more earnestly". As mature Christians we must recognise the fact that we are in a spiritual battle, a battle between good and evil. The armour of the Christian is prayer in much the same way that Jesus prepared for His most supreme test—His crucifixion at Calvary. Jesus cried out to God in the Garden of Gethsemane "Father if thou be willing remove this cup from me, nevertheless not my will be done, but yours" (Luke 22:42). The Bible says in that awesome moment Christ "prayed more earnestly" to the extent that "great drops of blood" fell from His body.

I lost count of the many prayer meetings we had in Romania to counteract adversity and persecution during our time there. The saints of God congregated and cried unto God and God continually heard those cries and delivered us out of the hands of our enemies. I lost count, too, of periods when people would attack our faith and we had to bark back at them in the Spirit. As John Calvin wrote "If a dog barks when his master is attacked, how can I stand and do nothing when my Master is being reviled?" Sometimes we must take our stand in prayer. Merely crying out to God doesn't always ensure we get our desire, of course, but it guarantees that we find God's will for our lives which is far better. The book of Jeremiah speaks of God's great ability to answer every prayer with the words "Call unto me and I will answer you and show you great and mighty things which you do not know". (Jeremiah 33:3). And again in the book of Psalms we are told "Call upon me in the day of trouble and I will answer you" (Psalm 50:15). Billy Graham once said "How sad that heaven is full of answers to prayer for which no one bothered to ask". Whatever situation you are in, keep praying persistently and lovingly until the Master hears and answers your heart-felt cries. His love is such that He could never turn away from such a call. His delight is to meet you and greet you at the point of your need. The Bible says "I cried to Him with my mouth and high praise was on my tongue" (Psalm 66:17).We must pray with our eyes on God, not on the difficulties we face. If we do this God's inner love far exceeds our most helpless call. If we were touched by the cry of a child in great need at night or responded to the bark of our dog for attention, how much more does the Father in heaven wait to answer the cries of His own children who desire to be in His lovely presence? Jesus said: "If you then being evil know how to give good gifts unto your children, how much more will your Father who is in heaven give good gifts to those who ask Him" (Matthew 7:11).

If you want to attract God's attention, don't be afraid to bark the odd prayer in the direction of heaven. Don't be afraid to pray loudly unto God. He's such a good God He's just waiting and willing to respond.

CHAPTER FIFTEEN

FOLLOWING HIS MASTER

"Looking unto Jesus, the author and finisher of our faith"
(Hebrews 12:2).

LESSON 15—GOD LEADS AND WE FOLLOW.

If a puppy knows who his master is, then that puppy is a friend for life and will follow him thereafter wherever he goes. Indeed, if a dog is a man's best friend, as is often claimed, nowhere is this better illustrated than in the loyalty and obedience of Snowbell. For once Snowbell became familiar with his own master he, too, would follow no matter where I would go. When I approached the forecourt of our house, guess who would be there right behind me? If I would turn unexpectedly and walk the other way, Snowbell would spin around in a circle and get in step behind me. He was like a little sticking plaster, one that just couldn't be separated from me. It was almost as if he was just waiting on his next command to go and fetch something, or even for his daily play time to arrive, when I would interact with him with a stick or ball or some other toy he was accustomed to. Of course, that's not to say that Snowbell was born obedient or knew from a puppy how to follow his master. It took some time for him to yield not just to myself, but others in the house whom he would identify with as being in charge.

I will never forget the day I watched him following one of the security men outside. I was standing on the third floor of our house looking out of the window and had the most vivid view of what was taking place down below. The security man was just pacing up and down through utter boredom, but Snowbell seemed to have his own mission to complete. He just kept in step with the guard no matter where the guard would go. When he stopped, Snowbell stopped. When the man took off again Snowbell followed immediately. It was so comical, yet a far cry from when he first arrived at our house and ran wild around the garden subject to no-one. Through study I have been educated much about how male Labradors like Snowbell are favoured as helpful, obedient and socially well adapted and loyal companions, especially by older and disabled people. Their winning, good-natured dispositions and general friendliness to all comers makes it easier for owners to take them into public places like supermarkets, shops and streets. These qualities are extremely important in public sector working dogs such as police canine units, and in serving the needs of individuals. Bad tempered dogs and disobedient dogs only add to the burden of age or disability. A reliable temperament and total obedience is a vital quality in any service animal, which must deal with all kinds of situations and with a variety of persons.

When the children first arrived at the home they were extremely undisciplined in lots of ways. Some were even jumping out of windows and the place resembled a zoo instead of a children's home. Thanks to the efforts of Mama Louise and the rest of the staff who worked night and day with our kids, over time that all changed and even the child protection officers were stunned at the transformation of certain children who had previously proven a problem elsewhere. What was the difference, then? One word—discipline! Children need boundaries and so, too, did Snowbell. Like all dogs he needed to be trained and, in this respect, thanks to modern day techniques, dogs like Snowbell now have the perfect assistance for such training. In order to help train a Labrador properly a top veterinarian, Professor Bob Anderson and Ruth Anderson, a former President of the National Association of Obedience Instructors, developed what is today known as "The Gentle Leader system". First launched in the 1980's the Gentle Leader is a comfortable nylon head collar designed specifically for dogs like Snowbell. It can be used on any dog for that matter and fits the contours of each individual dog's face. It's a quite fascinating scientific system in the control, management and training of dogs. Dogs like Snowbell have a natural instinct to pull against pressure meaning they choke on a regular collar. On the other hand, the Gentle Leader does not choke the dog. Instead it is designed to direct the dog's entire body by controlling his head and nose, in the same way man for centuries has controlled horses, camels, sheep and other livestock. Dogs of any age respond instinctively with relaxed subordination when their leader gently grasps their muzzle.

This is when the dog becomes a picture of what God intended every Christian to be once they have agreed to make the Lord Jesus Christ the master of their own lives. One day while sitting at his office Matthew the tax collector met with Jesus. The first instruction Christ gave Matthew was: "Follow me" and the Bible records that immediately Matthew arose and followed Him. When Christ met fishermen He gave them a similar command, saying, "Come follow Me and I will make you fishers of men." The original Greek meaning of this verse is, "Come follow Me and I will make you to 'become' fishers of men". The greatest success quality on earth is the willingness to become. How interesting that the original translation has included this word "become". Just as Snowbell had to learn to follow me, so the Christian life takes similar training, discipline and patience before we "become" what God intended us to be. The more the Christian yields to God's Holy Spirit the better they become at following their master. Subsequently we become subordinate and sensitive to the leading of our master, one who is not harsh, but gentle in every respect. If you have heard that He is a hard Master to serve this is simply not the case. The Saviour is full of love, mercy and incredible patience. His is the ultimate "gentle leader" system.

The youngest child we cared for at Carani was just 3 years old when she arrived. Naturally it wasn't long before she and Mama Louise became inseparable. I still marvel at how this little girl totally trusted Louise, taking her hand and following her every move. Many of us need to get back to that same place with God. We need to get back to a place where we just simply, with a child-like faith, trust God to lead us every day. Trust Him to lead us to pastures green, pastures new and pastures so pleasant. Notwithstanding, our flesh may still desire to resist such leadership, but the Spirit of the Lord facilitates us to follow our leader wherever He may go. How do we know this? Paul writing to the Romans said "Where sin abounds, therefore doth grace abound even more" (Romans 5:20). God's grace and gentle leading enables all of us to succumb to such authority, which we eventually find a most rewarding experience. Jesus said: "If any man serve me let him follow me and where I am there shall also my servant be. If any man serves me, him will my Father honour" (John 12:26). In the book of Matthew, Jesus espoused the benefits of his own Gentle Leader system with the words: "Come unto me all ye that labour and are heavy laden and I will give you rest. Take my yoke upon you and learn of me for I am meek and lowly in heart and you will find rest unto your souls. For my yoke is easy and my burden is light". The book of Proverbs states "the way of the transgressor is hard"; on the contrary, the way of God is easy. Christ does not force us to choke on the bad things in life. His guidance is gentle and kind or, as Samuel wrote in the Old Testament, "As for God, His way is perfect" (2 Samuel 22:31).

There is great comfort to be found in the leadership of Jesus. Of course, following Christ is essential if one aspires to live the Christian life. It is impossible to claim to be a Christian and yet refuse to follow the leading of the Lord or the leading of the Holy Spirit. This was especially emphasized in the gospels when the Lord appeared to indicate to some of His first disciples that the main requirement to being a Christian was to follow in obedience after Him. Obedience is doing anything God commands of you regardless of the cost of the consequences. Obedience is proof of our love for God, yet obeying God doesn't always appear logical to the natural mind of man. We regularly question God's instructions to us and even refuse to carry them out for fear of making a fool of ourselves. Obedience is doing what God requires even when it doesn't seem to make sense.

When we are at the right place of obedience the right people begin to enter our lives. Provision is also guaranteed at the place of obedience. While disobedience can often bring the chastening of God, obedience brings His blessing. Promotion always follows our obedience to God and brings us closer to God. Mike Murdock writes "Your obedience is the miracle magnet that keeps the presence of God around you". In John chapter 2 which records the story of Christ's first recorded miracle when, at a wedding, He turned water into wine, we are told He asked the servants to fill six water pots of stone with water. It seemed like an unusual request, yet Mary, His mother, said unto the curious servants "Whatsoever he saith unto you, do it" (John 2:5). It didn't seem logical, but wine came from that water, the best of wine, which Christ had kept until the end.

In the Old Testament a King called Naaman, who suffered from leprosy, was told by God's anointed servant Elisha to go and dip in the river Jordan 7 times. Again the request didn't make sense, it was even embarrassing and awkward for the King, but when Naaman obeyed God's Word and his servant the Bible says he was not only healed of his leprosy, his flesh also came again like unto the flesh of a little child. In another account, when the water dried up and the Word of the Lord came to Elijah and told him to turn eastward to the Brook Cherith, before Jordan, it didn't make sense to God's anointed servant. Why? Elijah was told by God that he would be fed by the most gluttonous bird on the planet, the raven, something which must have made him laugh. Yet after he obeyed God this ravenous fowl brought God's servant bread and flesh in the morning and bread and flesh in the evening and he drank of the brook also. While others were starving and dying of thirst, obedience brought a blessing of provision in the life of Elijah. When the disciples had been out fishing all night and caught nothing, Jesus told them to let down their nets again for a draught. These were experienced fishermen, who knew that if they hadn't managed to catch any fish at night, they certainly were not going to catch any the following morning. Nevertheless, the disciples did as Christ bade them and they hadn't enough room in the nets to contain the fish that were eventually caught. "And Simon answering said unto his Master: we have toiled all night and taken nothing; nevertheless at thy word I will let down the net. And when they had done this they enclosed a great multitude of fishes and their net brake" (Luke 5:6-7).What am I saying? Obedience produces miracles. In the book of Luke we are told of His disciples that "They forsook all and followed Him" (Luke 5:11). They heard God's voice and immediately obeyed the command to follow Him. Even in the Old Testament Caleb was a man who followed the Lord with all of his heart. Whatever his Master told him to do he did it.

One day I was out for a walk with Snowbell when not far from the house, he refused to respond to my instruction to catch up with me. He slipped off down a lane and appeared to be missing until I saw him sprinting away towards the main road. Frantically, I called and called after him, but he didn't even look back. I realised that if he didn't stop quickly he could easily be knocked down by the passing traffic. As it happened he was most fortunate, because not only did he fail to stop, there was no traffic on the road at that time and he made it safely over to the other side of the road. The consequences of not obeying the voice of his master, however, could have been fatal.

The biggest mistake we can make is to get off course in our Christian lives by disobeying God's voice. In Matthew chapter 14 Peter the apostle was commanded by Christ to get into a boat and "go to the other side". Instead the big fisherman temporarily took his eyes of the Lord and stepped out unto the water and "began to sink". I have concluded that the enemy will do anything to prevent us from carrying out God's original instruction in our lives. He will allow us to become involved in any cause other than the one God intended for us and he can even accept a miracle like walking on the water for a short time, as Peter experienced. Therefore following after God is to focus upon God carefully every day and upon what He wants and not what we want or even view as important. As Paul writes in the book of Hebrews "Looking unto Jesus, the author and finisher of our faith". The beauty of the story in Matthew chapter 14 is that it still produced a happy ending. Christ stretched out His hand and saved Peter. The boat not only made it to the other side, but great miracles were also wrought there. I, too, felt the touch of the master's hand on more than one occasion in Romania. How many times did He stretch out and pull me up from the brink of despair? How many times did I attempt to go the wrong way and veer down the wrong path, but the shepherd pulled his sheep back into line just when disaster was about to strike. God by His grace allows you and I to sink and swim during a season of practical growth, but He never leaves our side. He got us back on course many times and gave us victories which had previously seemed impossible. He even used the love of a dog to remind me that the Father's love is the greatest and most prevailing of all loves—the love of God Himself.

Of course, while God will give us the grace to follow, that's not to suggest the road is still not paved with pitfalls and times of discomfort. The Christian life is not always a bed of roses. There are lonely seasons, too, when the Christian may be in want waiting for the next instruction, yet there are spells when great joy and rest prevails. God is a good God. At times in Romania I felt at breaking point, but suddenly the peace of God returned to my life and His Hand led the way. His leading is balanced and never takes us beyond what we can bear and there is great reward for those who endure.

There are many thorns along the way as we take our stand for truth and righteousness. Christ said "He that takes not up his cross and follows after me cannot be my disciple" (Matthew 10:38). Following Christ in the good times and in the bad is the true face of Christianity. Being one step behind our Lord and never in front is also the mark of the successful Christian. Being willing to identify with Him in both prosperous times and periods of persecution is the real call of the following Christian.

Prior to Christ's crucifixion a certain man came to Jesus and proclaimed: "Master, I will follow you wherever you go", but Christ gave him an interesting reply, some may even venture to call it a reality check, answering: "The foxes have holes and the birds of the air have nests, but the Son of Man has nowhere to lay his head" (Matthew 8:20). What a challenge this was to this individual! Jesus was warning this man that while Christianity is a victorious life the price attached to it is a cross and that cross is often obedience.

I have found that to ignore God is to plan a disaster. Disobedience is always more costly than obedience. The Bible tells us that "Obedience is better than sacrifice" (I Samuel 15:22).

When my life was experiencing seasons of blessings, Snowbell would walk slowly behind me; equally when I was anxious or troubled, when life's storms had set in, it was as if he sensed this and drew even closer. He never overtook me, but you knew he was very near. He couldn't, of course, ask where I was taking him; instead he would implicitly trust my leading and my judgement. How similar is the life of the Christian who aspires to follow Christ. Following our Master is, as Solomon wrote, to "Trust in the Lord with all your heart and lean not unto your own understanding" (Proverbs 3:5). A favourite hymn of mine goes "Where He will lead me I will go, for I have learned to trust Him so, knowing someday that I shall see Jesus my friend of Calvary".

I led and Snowbell followed. In the Christian life God leads and we follow—that's simply how it's meant to be. In short, the instruction we follow determines the very future we create.

Chapter Sixteen

Sheltering from the Storm

"He that dwells in the secret place of the most high God shall abide under the shadow of the Almighty" (Psalm 91).

Lesson 16—Never try to fight the enemy on your own.

Romanian summers are renowned for being stiflingly hot, particularly Western Romania. It can reach as high as 44C and the intense heat can be difficult to endure. Of course, anything beyond 30C is hot enough for most of us, including Snowbell, who was a master at taking cover out of the constant blazing summer sun. On those hot days I noticed Snowbell beginning to get restless. He would twist from side to side, roll over and scratch his tummy and ears. Then, like normal, he'd leave us and amble into the hallway of our school classroom which, despite the soaring temperatures outside, still managed to remain cool. I would watch him spread himself upon the ground and within no time a deep peaceful sleep would come over him. At that moment our dog resembled probably the safest, most contented animal in the entire world. While others were baking outside, Snowbell was chilling inside. He only reappeared if there was an extreme emergency such as collecting his daily food offering or perhaps to chase some poor little bird off the premises. The pattern was similar in winter time, too. When the bitter eastern European winds would arrive followed by lashing rain and snow, Snowbell was tucked up comfortably in his bed. Even during the spring and summer storms which came our way frequently, Snowbell knew how to dive for cover when the elements turned against him. I would observe how he would immediately retreat to his hut and take shelter from the storm, not emerging until the threat of injury or harm was well and truly over.

Naturally at times he was clearly frightened, especially during the powerful bouts of thunder and lightning which Romania can experience. He wasn't the only one, mind you. I too used to hide in the cupboards and underneath the bed and pray until those violent storms were over. They were unlike anything I'd ever witnessed. In fact, the children used to joke that while I would pray for the storm to pass, they were praying for me.

I recall an incident, however, when all of us thought we had lost Snowbell for good during a violent storm. It was a dark black day and the skies had been threatening rain all morning. Instead, a wind storm caught us all by surprise before the expected downpour erupted. Unusually, our gate had been left open and Snowbell managed to escape. Once the wind began to gust through the village he lost his way and became totally disoriented. I charged out of the house accompanied by others to look for him. We called out his name loudly, but there was no response. I immediately panicked at the thought of losing him. It was actually one of the first indications of how close I'd grown to Snowbell. The idea of living without him was something I hadn't previously contemplated and I was all too aware of how dogs frequently became lost in Romania. Now I considered the fact that my dog may have joined that list. Thankfully and mercifully, however, we found him just in time. Not in the streets where we'd been looking, mind you, but standing pitifully outside the gate of the home. Despite the strong gale Snowbell had managed to find his way back to the home and, wouldn't you know it, he began barking excitedly when he saw us all running up the street. That was the only time I remember him venturing outside when a storm was at its height and it may just have taught him and us a great lesson. Instead, during nasty weather interruptions, Snowbell always remained confident that the spot which he had chosen to hide was indeed secure, a behavioural pattern which readily reminded me of much of my own Christian life. During times of extreme pressure I have had to run for cover from the bitter elements of life. On occasions when I haven't done so, it's proved a painful experience. Isn't it good to know that there is somewhere reliable where all of us can run to when things are tough and when the gales of life begin to blow against us? Throughout these periods I've called frantically unto God and asked for His protection until the danger was well and truly ended. Many times I've locked myself in God's cupboards, hiding and praying underneath His wings until calm has returned. Such provision, however, is only promised to those who know Christ as their personal Saviour and make Him their daily source of strength and help. In many respects, Snowbell was a picture of how to live a victorious Christian life, a wonderful example of wisdom and trust. The wisest thing we can do when adversity strikes is to seek the Lord for His great covering. Psalm 91 declares "He that dwells in the secret place of the most high God shall abide under the shadow of the Almighty". This is a powerful psalm in its entirety describing Almighty God as a fortress and a refuge, no less. The psalm tells us that when we take cover in Him we are promised no fear of the terror of night, nor of the arrow which flies by day. The writer adds that while thousands will fall around us, due to severe set-backs in their own lives, none of these calamities will come near the man or woman who trusts in God and makes Him their dwelling place.

In a world which is changing constantly and facing crisis after crisis, how wonderful it is to know that Jesus is still the rock in a weary land—a shelter in a time of storm! He commands His angels to guard us, promises to be with us in trouble and even extends to us the privilege of long life.

Many times when trouble came our way in Romania it became almost second nature to retreat to the place of prayer. Our church would often be used as a hiding place to ask for God's covering against the forces of darkness. Visitations by Child Protection officers and Romanian authorities in general used to be dreaded by me and Louise and our staff due to the apparent prejudice towards our home. Unnecessary and unjustifiable fines could be imposed and other difficult measures would often materialise meaning we were constantly in a state of prayer and at times fasting.

In the book of Exodus Moses told the children of Israel that, despite the presence of a death angel, God would not allow any harm to come their way because blood was sprinkled upon their homes; instead, the death angel would pass over them and they would be protected. This is not merely an ancient Bible story, God did this many times for us in Romania and He's still doing this for His children today.

Just recently a friend of mine in the land of Kenya, who lives with her young daughter, told me a story which clearly illustrates God's wonderful protection from the storms of life. She had asked me to personally pray for her every day, something which I had being doing for several months. One night this lady was woken by the sound of gunfire and shouting and discovered that a gang of men were running in and out of the houses close to where she lived. When they broke into her house the leader of the group said that he felt very uncomfortable. He told the others to leave immediately. A serving Christian, this lady was rejoicing for she knew that her house had been covered by the precious blood of Jesus. The prayers of God's people had protected both her and her daughter when they were most in need. Even the demons recognised the anointing of God. The New Testament offers our generation the same divine care as was offered to Moses and the children of Israel in the Old Testament and this through the blood of Jesus Christ. His blood is our sword and shield; it protects and covers us as we experience life's storms. The Bible says we "overcome him (that is, the devil) by the word of our testimony and by the blood of the lamb" (Revelation 12:11). Despite this provision, it's amazing how many Christians still choose to do their own thing; how they yet prefer to try and operate in the harshest of conditions when they could have the shelter of God Himself. If we are to overcome the world, the flesh and the devil, we must have Christ's assistance. Jesus told His disciples "Behold I give unto you power to tread on serpents and scorpions and over all the power of the enemy and nothing shall by any means hurt you" (Luke 10:19).

In one of his greatest ever parables the Lord Jesus warned about the folly of building our Christian lives upon shaky and unreliable foundations. He likened it to building upon sand which the wind would eventually blow away. Instead He exhorted us to build upon the rock which never changes, Christ Himself. The Lord Jesus said, "Everyone who hears these words of mine and does them, I will liken him to a wise man, who built his house upon a rock. The rain came down, the floods came, and the winds blew, and beat on that house, but it did not fall for it was founded upon the rock." Then He added "Everyone who hears these words of mine and doesn't do them will be like a foolish man, who built his house on sand.

The rain came down, the floods came and the winds blew and beat on that house; and it fell—and great was its fall" (Matthew 7 24-27). This parable emphasises the need to put Christ's teachings into practice and speaks of two sorts of people whose hearts are revealed by their actions. Rain, floods and winds metaphorically expresses calamities and afflictions which befall men in life, but if we are founded upon the rock none of these will cause us to stumble and fall. It's possible to lose your spouse, your job, your house and, yes, you may even lose a ministry, but if your hope is in Christ, your faith will survive the worst of those same storms. Our relationship with the "work of the Lord" is not as important as our relationship with the "Lord of the work".

The world is currently being blown away by storms of unprecedented nature. There are, of course, physical storms such as floods, hurricanes, earthquakes, tsunamis, etc, which are causing great harm to our natural habitat, but other storms have appeared too like the global economic crisis which has affected virtually every country. The church has been rocked in recent years due to scandals of all kinds and things we once "put our house on" so-to-speak have collapsed before our very eyes. Men used to depend on banks for the safety of their money and upon the church for the security of their faith. Not anymore. Therefore those without a relationship with God are destined to flounder amidst all of the uncertainty being experienced in our world today. During times like these there is only one place to run to—the safety of the presence of God. When the disciples found themselves caught in that nasty storm mentioned in the previous chapter, the book of Matthew records that Peter beginning to sink quickly cried out "Lord save me". It was a cry that was immediately heard by Jesus who stretched forth his hand and caught him and said "How little faith you have; why did you doubt?" We are then told that the wind ceased and those who witnessed the incident said to Jesus: "Of a truth art not thou the Son of God!" (Matthew 14-30-33).

Have you ever faced storms in your life? Times when things just didn't make sense? Your problems appeared so vast and your faith so small. Times when you feared you wouldn't make it, so swamped you believed the storms were going to overtake you. The disciples were not really any different in Bible days. They, too, encountered storms and learned great lessons from them. They learned that no matter how well life can seemingly be going, storms do come and only those with faith in Christ are prepared for such inclement weather. It only takes a second for a storm to arrive and for everything to come crashing down around us. The loss of a job, a family member becomes terminally ill, a natural disaster hits your home or a wife or husband decides to have an affair thus leaving a family devastated.

These days, financial experts reckon most people are less than three missed mortgage payments away from bankruptcy. Imagine, less than three months away from financial meltdown! Of course, in the case of the disciples, it wasn't a spiritual storm, but a physical one. Nevertheless the principle is similar. No doubt when the disciples set out the weather was fine, but in no time waves were coming over the boat and fear enveloped them. I know how they must have felt. I recall going out on a boat on the Sea of Galilee during the late 1990's. It was so calm and beautiful when we set out, but we ended up needing help on our return when a really strong gale got up and the boat became very unsafe. I, too, remember getting anxious as were many others on that boat. Then I considered how the disciples were themselves caught in a violent storm and became fearful. It became so bad, the disciples addressed Christ as "teacher" or "Master" saying "do you not care that we perish?" Is that any different to the question being asked by millions of people today? They cannot cope and so they ask God "What's going on, have you forgotten us, have you given up on us?" If we really understood God's great care and love for us we would never insult our Creator with such a question. Take a handful of sand and count the grains, then take a bucket full and count it, then take a beach and count the grains. Then gather all the sand in the entire world and count it. It would be easy to give up, wouldn't it? Yet God has never given up on you and is thinking and praying for you right now as you read this book. "How precious also are thy thoughts unto me, Oh God! How great is the sum of them! If I should count them, they are more in number than the sand" (Psalm 139:17:18).

God loves you and the Lord has not forgotten any of His children; moreover He's right there in the midst of the storm with His children. Storms come, yes, but guess what? Storms go also. Storms settle down and especially when Christ speaks to them for us. In the book of Mark Jesus simply rebuked the wind and the waves saying "peace be still" and we are told the wind ceased and there was a great calm. But Jesus had a question for His disciples saying "how is it that you are so fearful?" (Mark 4:40). In other words, God wants us to trust Him in the good times and in the bad. He is pleased when we show faith in the storms of life and remain focused on Him. When I was a member of the Boy's Brigade our motto was "sure and steadfast". Our favourite hymn was entitled "Will your anchor hold?" It was about God's certainty and about the security of having Christ as an anchor in our lives. It goes "Will your anchor hold in the storms of life, when the clouds unfold their wings of strife, when the strong tides lift and the cables strain, will your anchor drift or firm remain. We have an anchor that keeps the soul, steadfast and sure while the billows roll, fastened to the rock which cannot move, grounded firm and deep in the Saviour's love".

If a dog has the sense to take shelter from the storms of life how much more should we also run to the strong tower that is Christ when times are hard. Snowbell simply refused to fight the elements in his own strength. He knew he couldn't do this. Taking cover when the tide of life is against us is to truly trust God and His strength to see us through. "So this is what the sovereign Lord says, see I lay a stone in Zion, a tested stone, a precious cornerstone for sure foundation, the one who trusts will never be dismayed" (Isaiah 28:16).

If we call upon God in the day of trouble He will deliver us, this is God's certain promise to us. Jesus said: "Let not your heart be troubled, you believe in God, believe also in me" (John 14:1). We, like Snowbell, must retreat to the shelter and to the house that is steadfast and sure. Edward Mote wrote in his great hymn "My hope is built on nothing less, than Jesu's blood and righteousness, I dare not trust the sweetest frame but wholly trust in Jesu's name, on Christ the solid rock I stand, all other ground is sinking sand, all other ground is sinking sand".

So, there is no excuse for feeling too hot, too cold or even downright weather-beaten. Christ has already provided a safe haven for us to hide in. He did it constantly for us in Romania and He can do it for you. All you need to do is amble in like Snowbell, lie down for a while and wait until the tempest has dispersed. Never, ever, try and fight the enemy on your own.

CHAPTER SEVENTEEN

THE GREATEST LOVE OF ALL

"Behold what manner of love the Father has bestowed
upon us" (1 John 3:1).

LESSON 17—LOVE NEVER FAILS . . . .

Have you ever ended up loving someone whom at first you couldn't
stand? It happens to us all. We meet people who, for whatever
reason, seem to initially get on our nerves. We avoid them like
the plague and speak negatively about them when they're not around. Then
something happens which begins to pierce the walls of prejudice we've
wrongly built up against them. They start to reach out to us in a way we
didn't expect. At first this gesture of friendship is rejected, but it keeps
coming and eventually there is no alternative but to respond to these silent,
yet powerful overtures of love. In the end we become best friends with a
person we once deeply disliked and, instead of regaling them, we are first
to defend them at every opportunity and wonder how we even got along
without them for so long.

It can happen with animals also for this was unquestionably my experience
with Snowbell. Years of prejudice towards dogs and a determination not
to even allow him into our own home in Romania proved no match for
Snowbell's loving instinct and the great depth of love he would eventually
show to me. I must confess that over the years he gate-crashed our house on

numerous occasions, much to my delight. He couldn't make my dinner or bring me flowers, although I often wondered was that what he was trying to do when he dug up the backyard flowerbed. Yet he brought me a love I never thought possible.

Many accounts of his gentle and placid nature lie deep within my memory bank, but perhaps the greatest is the incredulous tale of how he once tried to barricade me in when I was attempting to leave for a holiday. I had just come down the stairs of the Children's House with a large suitcase which I intended to put into the car. Walking the entire way along the forecourt Snowbell tried to block my path, eventually lying down in front of the case. Initially I wondered what he was doing. He clearly wasn't playing because he appeared more than a trifle sad. I was genuinely bemused as to what was wrong with him. Then suddenly it dawned on me that this beautiful little dog may have been trying, in his own way, to convey the message that he didn't want me to leave. If he could have eaten my passport I believe he would have. At that point I recall my eyes filling up with tears. Had the holiday not already been booked and paid for I would gladly have stayed at home and given him what he wanted. It was an expression of love and a precious moment that still touches my heart even to this day.

They say the reason a dog has so many friends is because he wags his tail instead of his tongue. How true with Snowbell. If ever his loving and beautiful nature was exposed to me it was in that very moment. He loved our interaction and communication and didn't want to live without it, even for a couple of weeks. "Can you imagine that?" commented my equally speechless secretary Lacramioara, as she watched the dog bark and fight with me in the grounds of our home. By now his love had simply overwhelmed all of us and we had no resistance to it. The truth is he was so beautiful and irresistible he made all of us love him. Human relationships break up, but a dog will never leave you. Imagine if you were on a dating website and saw a profile of someone who promised to be the most loyal companion ever, would reduce your stress levels and would always be happy to see you. It would probably seem too good to be true, wouldn't it? Yet Snowbell possessed all of these qualities. His was a love that tunnelled through all of my own preconceived notions about dogs; a love so infectious that even today I am left flabbergasted at just how this little dog managed to radically change my heart and life. Love is immeasurable! Why? Because love heals, it cures people—both the ones who give it and the ones who receive it. I gave Snowbell time I could spare, space I could spare and love I could spare. In return this beautiful Labrador gave me his all. My goal in life from that point on was to try and be as good a person as Snowbell viewed me.

When he followed me every step of the way he was saying "I love you". When he lay down beside me and comforted me having sensed my discouragement he was saying "I love you". When he interacted with me and played games and shared in my joy, he was saying "I love you". When he barked at people whom he recognised were giving me a hard time and showed his protective nature he was simply saying "I love you". When he barked up at our window in the morning and barked at others who were getting "too much attention" he was saying in his own little way "I love you". His love became irresistible and it was as though he could see only the good in me. What a dog and what a friend Snowbell had become to me! Solomon wrote "A friend loveth at all times and a brother is born for adversity" (Proverbs 17:17). In an even greater way, of course, our Lord Jesus Christ has displayed a level of love to the world that is, in itself, so infinite and so powerful, many hearts have been touched by it and countless lives have been totally transformed.

Christ too has fought with multitudes for their affections and demonstrated that His greatest desire is to have daily communion with His own creation. He too gives us a sense of worth and sees only the best in us. Christ's love for us is so enormous and so unconditional; it's a depth of love beyond our comprehension. When we are exposed to this love we have no alternative but to love him in return. As John wrote "We love him, because he first loved us". (1 John 4:19). Arguably the most quoted verse of scripture illustrates best the depth of God's great love for mankind. "For God so loved the world that he gave his only begotten Son, that whosoever believes in him shall not perish, but shall have everlasting life" (John 3:16). Many opposed to God and His Kingdom have instead become some of God's greatest exponents on behalf of the gospel of Jesus Christ. Take Saul as an example. Here was a man in the New Testament who the Bible says "wasted the church", yet ultimately became Paul the great apostle after being challenged on the Damascus road by God's great love. If evidence is required of how God's love can transform even His most bitter enemies then this particular conversion is sufficient. Regardless of the suffering and pain and great sacrifice involved in this act of love, demonstrated to obtain the forgiveness of our sins, many still do not initially accept the love of God; instead they reject it and even speak wickedly against it.

I still recall the days when Snowbell first came to our house. He would snuggle up beside me looking for attention. Cruelly I would push him out of the way in a macho manner; refusing to accept the great comfort this dog was capable of giving. I naively assumed I didn't need his love and even believed he couldn't win my love for him. But he never gave up and never changed his loving nature towards me. Just as Snowbell continued to love me with great affection, even when I would blatantly shun him, Christ too loves us when we are clearly unworthy of such love and remain alien to Him. How many have done the same thing when it comes to the love of God! How many millions have pushed God away assuming they can live without His love in this world, all the time not realising that His love is exactly the thing they require, a beautiful, kind and amazing love that has the power to alter their very lives. We may not believe in God, but God constantly believes in us. Paul writes in Romans: "But God commended his love towards us in that while we were yet sinners, Christ died for us" (Romans 5:8). And again writing in the book of Ephesians he adds: "But God who is rich in mercy, for His great love wherewith he has loved us" Ephesians 2:4). This kind of love is irresistible. It breaks down every barrier and can mend every broken heart. It wasn't someone preaching to me constantly that changed my opinion about dogs, nor was it a sudden desire to become more animal friendly. The outstanding difference in me becoming a dog lover instead of someone who disliked dogs was the love shown to me by a dog, the powerful love that Snowbell penetrated my life with. So it is with God. Love is the real reason why men and women are drawn to Christ. Love is the answer to difficult and unlikeable people in our lives. It is not the fear of hell that prompts many to repent of their sins and seek God's great forgiveness, contrary to popular opinion. It's not hatred and strife that conquers over the issues of life and wins their hearts. The Bible says it is the "goodness of God that leads one to repent" (Romans 2:4).

When people finally grasp the loveliness of the King; when they understand the enormity of His sacrifice at Calvary and acknowledge the love behind the suffering there, this is what finally transforms a cynical sinner into a thankful saint. Paul also states that "love endures long, is patient and kind ". What a wonderful picture of the love and mercy of God this is! Psalm 145 says "For the Lord is gracious and full of compassion, slow to anger and of great mercy". Here we see the greatest love of all. Love is the very essence of the gospel story. We hear so much these days about the God of judgement and God certainly is the final judge of all the earth; nevertheless the true nature of God is to love and display the mercy that a broken world such as ours so demands. John writes: "Behold what manner of love the Father has bestowed upon us" (1 John 3:1). The word "behold" in this context means "look". In other words John is saying look at how immense God's love is for His creation".

When we originally came to Romania the children were naturally sceptical about us; some were understandably quite cold towards us. During their short but troubled lives, they had many people coming and staying for a week or a month, then leaving to do something else. We on the other hand had made a commitment to God on their behalf to stay with them for as long as possible. During almost a decade in Romania, we just kept on loving them, no matter how they responded initially and, in time, the barriers began to fall. Over the years all of the children, even the most stubborn ones, learned to trust us. Once they knew for certain they were loved by us, guess what happened? They began to love us in return. In the end we became a tightly knit family full of love and happiness. God's greatest desire is simply that we would love Him back and become a part of his family. Isn't that amazing! The God of the universe, the one who created the sun, moon and stars, wants us to love Him. In the book of Revelation, addressing the church at Ephesus, Christ rebuked this church despite the fact that they had been found faithful in many areas. Why? Because they stopped loving Him. "Nevertheless I have somewhat against you, because you have left your first love" (Revelation 2:4). This was a call to cold Christians, more interested in doing God's work than loving the God of the work. Dr. James Moffatt translates this verse as "You have given up loving me as you did at the first". God is after our love as well as our works and when He gets this love, and gives us His in return, we can do anything and we can change any closed heart toward us. Christ once asked the apostle Peter no fewer than three times, "Do you love me?" Imagine the Creator of the universe interested in the love of a fisherman? What does this say about the heart of God towards His creation? The Bible says of Jacob "And Jacob served seven years for Rachel and they seemed unto him but a few days because of the love he had for her" (Genesis 29:20). God wants Christians to use the most powerful force on earth—love. The love of Christ enables missionaries to endure emotional battles, financial difficulties and cultural barriers in their ministries among the heathen. Wives have helped in the process of their husbands' salvation through prayer and love. Love pursues, protects and provides.

In the First book of Corinthians, known as "the love chapter of the Bible," Paul the apostle states "Love never fails, but whether there be prophecies, they shall fail; whether there be tongues, they shall cease; whether there be knowledge, it shall vanish away" (1 Corinthians 13:8-9). In other words Paul reminds us that love is the weapon that wins and changes people's hearts.

The Greek word for love is agape. There are many forms of love, but agape love refers to the love of God or Christ for humankind. In the New Testament it refers to the covenant love of God for humans, as well as the human reciprocal love for God. The term agape is rarely used in the ancient manuscripts but was used by early Christians to refer to the self-sacrificing love of God for humanity. CS Lewis in his book "The Four Loaves" used agape to describe what he believed was the highest level of love known to humanity—a selfless love, a love that was totally and passionately committed to the well-being of others. The Christian usage of the term agape comes almost directly from the canonical gospels account of the teachings of Jesus. When asked what was the "great commandment" Jesus replied "Thou shalt love the Lord thy God with all thy heart, with all thy soul and with all thy mind". This is the first and great commandment. And the second is like unto it, Thou shalt love thy neighbour as thyself. On these two commandments hang all the law and the prophets (Matthew 22-37:40). The King James Version of the Bible translates the word agape as "charity", which has a connotation of giving to the needs of those less fortunate. That's why, perhaps, Christian writers have described agape love as a form of love which is both unconditional and voluntary. Oh that Christians would understand fully the words of Christ "Love one another as I have loved you". We should ask ourselves "How has He loved me?" Do

I really love others the same way? Mother Theresa said "Unless this love is among us, we can kill ourselves with work, and it will only be work, not love. Work without love is slavery". She then added "I am a little pencil in the hands of a writing God, who is sending a love letter to the world". I have felt like this little pencil as I've struggled to do justice to the love of God in the writing of this book. Is there a greater love than God's? Who can fully explain such love? The lyrics of Fredrick M Lahman's hymn are: "Could we with ink the ocean fill, and where the skies of parchment made, were every stalk on earth a quill and every man a scribe by trade; to write the love of God above would drain the ocean dry, nor could the scroll contain the whole, though stretched from sky to sky, Oh, love of God, how rich and pure! How measureless and strong! It shall forevermore endure—the saints' and angels' song". When a survey was completed on what people required most in life the expected answers of more money, a better government, a happy marriage, peace and prosperity, etc, failed to materialise. Instead the number one thing people required to make it through this life was the need to be loved. Therefore as the apostle ends God's great love letter in 1 Corinthians 13 he declares that faith, hope and love are all important, but the greatest of these is love. In the same way that God is full of love and has won us to Himself through this love, it's good when we possess this same characteristic in our own lives. If we give all that we have to the poor in providing food and if we surrender our bodies to be burned or in order that we may glory, but have not love (that is the love of God in us) then we gain nothing (1 Corinthians 13:3). On the contrary, Christ commands us to love with the words "I give to you a new commandment that you should love one another. Just as I have loved you, so you too should love one another" (John 13:34). Christ added by this shall all men know that you are my disciples if you love one another" (John 13:35) or as Mother Teresa also stated "Let no one ever come to you without leaving better and happier. Be the living expression of God's kindness", she said.

In a similar way that Snowbell made me love him due to his beautiful, kind and winsome nature, so, too, it is the very beauty and winsomeness of our Lord Jesus Christ that has won the hearts of millions and this in spite of the stupendous claims about Himself. Christ was loveable in spite of His loyalty to truth and in spite of the trials He endured. His manner was always gracious and attractive and radiated His whole life. The magnetism of His kindness far outlasted the memory of His miracles. Unlike the dew passing under the heat of a burning sun, the moral beauty of Christ consistently never fades. His love is irresistible and He always sees the good in us. He makes us love Him and His love never fails.

CHAPTER EIGHTEEN

THE GREATEST SACRIFICE OF ALL

"The Son of man did not come to be served, but to serve and
to give his life a ransom for many" (Matthew 20:28)".

LESSON 18—SACRIFICE IS A PAINFUL PROCESS.

They say the hardest part of missionary work is not leaving, nor the
work itself, but returning. It becomes almost a greater sacrifice and
a bigger ordeal to try and readjust again to the country of one's
birth, than to acclimatise in the first place to a new culture and a strange
land. I now sense how true this is.

I can still remember the day when news broke how the EU had instructed
Romania to close all large children's homes and overpopulated orphanages.
It was news which naturally came as a great shock to us. Despite the fact
that we had been in the process of evaluating our future in Romania, even
so, the realisation that our time there seemed to be drawing to a close
sooner than we had anticipated wasn't easily received.

After almost a decade of missionary endeavour by our church in Carani,
the thought of leaving Romania and returning home was a very sad one.
This sudden change in legislation by the European Union and Romanian
government meant that we also had to begin a reintegration programme,
thus moving many of the children back with their natural families or with

suitable foster parents. Due to Romania's acceptance as part of the EU, it was seen as a necessary next step in terms of progress for the eastern European nation. Naturally it proved to be a very emotional time for Louise and I and indeed all of the children in our care. We had become incredibly attached to them and separation now seemed like a cruel and untimely intervention. We were informed that only homes with ten or less children could remain open which signalled the beginning of the end of our time in Romania, as our own home had been built to house a maximum of sixty children. The exodus would prove to be a long, slow and painful process for all involved, but a hugely necessary one in helping to solve the crisis involving homeless and wayward children in Romania, which was still a massive problem. Even though it effectively brought our own ministry to an end, I believe it was the right decision by the EU. Instead of months, however, this procedure would take some years to complete and wasn't exactly what Louise or I had envisaged doing when we first arrived in Romania full of longer term and much more positive plans. We had even extended the home during our time there; now it would be left empty and desolate. This didn't detract from the fact that the care the children had received was vital in their own troubled lives. The part we played in ensuring other vulnerable children were now better protected was also something which was extremely necessary.

Naturally over the years we had become exceptionally attached to many of the children and staff members, a fondness which was reciprocated by them. In truth, we didn't want to be parted. Many of our staff would have to find new jobs, which wouldn't be easy in Romania. The thought of returning home and resettling in Ireland was also a frightening prospect for both Louise and myself. Obviously we had to remain strong for the sake of the children; nevertheless hiding our emotions wasn't easy, especially when it came time for another child to leave our home. There were lots of tears and sad goodbyes and truthfully it was a horrible period in all of our lives. Those final hugs, however, were a beautiful evidence of the great love and bond between us all because even now, many years later, the pain of that separation hasn't gone away totally, but the memories of good times are constant.

There was, of course, another problem regarding our premature departures; what to do about Snowbell. We may have already managed to reintegrate the children, but with no definite address for us to reside at, taking

Snowbell back to Ireland wasn't straightforward. Starting off again in a small apartment was our plan, hardly the ideal place for a Labrador to live. This dog had become so used to the outdoors and to the large grounds we had at the Children's House, that to hold him prisoner inside with no garden or even yard to play in would undoubtedly have been a cruel and thoughtless act. Having studied the history of this wonderful dog, born to run and born for a mountain-top experience, I knew taking him back with us was not even an option. He would have been miserable and we just couldn't envisage that. So, as difficult a prospect as it seemed, we realised we would have to leave him in Romania. It proved a hard decision, but the correct one, especially when a beautiful family in our church came forward at exactly the right time looking for a dog just like ours. They already loved him and, having lost their own family dog, due to old age, were on the lookout for a replacement. He appeared drawn to them also because every time they visited the home and the church Snowbell would run towards them as though he was advertising himself as a good catch.

None of this covers the fact that Snowbell's departure still left me feeling distraught. I vividly recall the day he left us and how it broke my heart to watch his cute little face gazing out of the back of the car as it slowly pulled out of the driveway for the last time. Even though he had spent several weeks with his new family acclimatising to his new environment the thought of letting him go was still unthinkable. The idea of never seeing him again had me in pieces. It struck me how I would never again see him charging to answer the bell, or sitting in his hut with his little manipulative face. It occurred to me also how I may never again get the chance to feel his incredible love which had touched my life in so many ways. I would miss terribly his barking for attention each morning; his demonstration of jealousy when I didn't give him the interest he so craved and how I would miss the way in which he would return to thank me daily for his food or any other gift I would bring him. I would no doubt long also for the way he would walk behind me each day in total subservience and the infectious manner in which he used to snuggle up close expressing his wonderful love for me. Had I really become so attached to this animal that, at such a moment, my very heart felt like it had been ripped from me? The only way I can describe it is that it felt like the death of a dear loved one. It was bad enough losing the children from our lives, but losing a dog I never thought I was destined to love was equally devastating.

Only now do I truly sympathise with animal lovers everywhere who, having experienced the death of their faithful pets, are often left totally broken-hearted. In the past I may have even mocked such people and put their emotions down to gushing sentimentality. Now I knew otherwise. I tried desperately to keep my own feelings hidden, in the same way I had hidden my true emotions from the children when it came time for one of them to leave, yet no words can describe the pain I experienced the day Snowbell left our home. Even in the days which have followed, the ache hasn't been totally erased from my heart. It's not so much the goodbye that hurts; it's the flashbacks which follow. Hardly a day passes when I don't think of our wonderful Labrador retriever and the joy he brought to us all. Looking back it was a major step agreeing to let Snowbell remain in Romania while we flew on to the next chapter of our lives over 3,000 miles away. I had to think long and hard about parting with him and, even after the decision was made, I still didn't feel very comfortable about it. On reflection, it was a similar situation the day we left home in Ireland to work in the mission field in Romania back at the beginning of the new millennium. Much sacrifice had to be made then, too, but a greater cause often makes sacrifice an easier thing to accomplish. Some people even enquired "Why in the world are you going to waste your lives as missionaries?" Christian martyr Jim Elliot was asked the same question to which he replied "Don't forget you too are expending your life, and when the bubble has burst, what of eternal significance will you have to show for the years you have wasted". Or, as the great missionary David Livingstone wrote "If a commission by an earthly king is considered an honour, how can a commission by a Heavenly King be considered a sacrifice".

Now, almost a decade later, it still felt like sacrifice was going to have to be made. I was very conscious of the fact that I was not just leaving the children and Snowbell behind; I was separating from a culture and a people I had grown to love. I would miss terribly the beautiful decorative language that is Romanian. I would miss the laidback approach to life I had surprisingly gotten used to and yes, I would even miss signing my name hundreds of times like a celebrity! All of these sacrifices paled into insignificance compared to the greatest sacrifice of all, the one made by God Almighty in allowing His only Son Jesus Christ to die upon a cross at the place called Calvary. If it broke my heart to willingly part with the children and our loving family pet, if it appeared to cost me something to leave my birth land and spend years in a foreign country serving a nation I knew not, how much harder was it for God to give His own Son in order that His creation could be saved? Jesus was the "darling of His bosom", one who was sinless and perfect and in whom God was "well pleased", yet He still sacrificed His Son for our benefit. Mahatma Gandhi said "Jesus Christ was a man completely innocent, who offered himself as a sacrifice for the good of others, including his enemies and became the ransom of the world. It was a perfect act".

Sacrifice is not a concept that anyone really looks forward to; moreover most people do everything they can to avoid making sacrifices. We loathe letting go of even a small bit of what we love the most. I know a man in his early fifties, who has stored in his garage every single Action Man he received as a child. Numerous times he's been told to "throw them out" or "give them away", yet he just can't sacrifice them. I also struggle to part with suits and ties, which have become so precious to me; I have even given them names like the offspring of a family. It's been said that "self-preservation is the first law of nature, but self-sacrifice is the highest rule of grace". Aldous Huxley says "There's only one effectively redemptive sacrifice, the sacrifice of self-will to make room for the knowledge of God".

The Lord Jesus Christ was the opposite of how many of us choose to live our lives. In His human life He was all about sacrifice, His whole life was a sacrifice. His greatest sacrifice, however, was his sacrificial death at Calvary to forgive the sins of mankind. And Christ knew all about forgiveness. When men had done their worst to Him, he simply responded "Father, forgive them, for they know not what they do". (Luke 23:34). The cost of this wonderful forgiveness was the greatest act of sacrifice in the history of the world. The book of John records "Greater love has no man than this that he lay down his life for his friends" (John 15:13). His supreme offering of His sinless life paid the terrible price of mankind's sins for all time. The writer to the Hebrews says "For then must he often have suffered from the foundation of the world, but now once in the end of the world hath he appeared to put away sin by the sacrifice of himself". (Hebrews 9:26). Even at the age of twelve when He told His parents that "He must be about His Father's business" He was thinking of this sacrifice. He was conscious that He had come into the world to bear the sins of every man and woman and child and this must have been a heavy burden upon Him. Think about it! The expectation that on His shoulders rested the destinies of countless billions of people was a weighty cup only He could eventually accept. What a Saviour is Jesus Christ! Described by John the Baptist as "The lamb of God who takes away the sin of the world" (John 1:29), Christ was slain from the foundation of the world. Had He not been no one could have received redemption and forgiveness through the shedding of His precious blood. Peter says "Knowing that you were not redeemed with corruptible things such as silver and gold, but with the precious blood of Christ, as of a lamb without blemish and without spot". (1 Peter 1-18:19). Abraham was told by God in the Old Testament to "take now thy son, thine only son Isaac", with the intention of sacrificing him on an altar, but God found an animal to replace Isaac. When it came to His own Son, however, no substitute was found and Christ was crucified upon the cross. If sacrifice is a painful business to mankind, how much more painful was it to God Almighty in surrendering His only Son to die.

Christ's sacrifice had been prophesied in many parts of the Old Testament, not least in one of the opening statements in the book of Genesis. "And I will put enmity between you (the serpent, Satan) and the woman and between her seed and your seed. He shall bruise your head and you shall bruise his heel. (Genesis 3:15). Even Isaiah more than alluded to the suffering Christ would endure upon the cross with two powerful scriptures. "All we like sheep have gone astray, we have turned, every one, to his own way, and the Lord has laid the iniquity of us all upon him". (Isaiah 53:6). And again he adds "For he was wounded for our transgressions, bruised for our iniquities, the chastisement of our peace was upon him and with his stripes we are healed". (Isaiah 53:5).

Something which is not often considered, however, was how Christ sacrificed in His life as much as in His death. In his daily life He was the perfect example of His own words in Luke 6:31 "And as ye would that men should do to you, do ye also to them likewise". He also said, "The Son of man did not come to be served, but to serve and to give his life a ransom for many" (Matthew 20:28). He continually thought of the best interests of others. Did I desire to bring Snowbell home to Ireland with Louise and myself? Did I consider my own interests in having Snowbell around me every minute of every day? Of course, I did. I agonised over the decision, but in the end sacrifice had to be made in the better interests of the dog. Sacrifice is a painful business which is always made for the greater good of someone or something else. Yet never was there pain and agonising like Christ suffered both during and prior to the cross. The book of Luke reminds us that "being in agony He prayed more earnestly, and His sweat was as it were great drops of blood falling down to the ground" (Luke 22:44). He even asked God to remove the cup of suffering from Him as His humanity clashed with His divinity. Still Luke records, He was always thinking of the Father's will and the best interests of others, before himself "Father if thou be willing remove this cup from me, nevertheless, not my will, but thine be done". (Luke 22:42). In this great act of love, Jesus Christ became the most unselfish person who ever lived. His was the greatest sacrifice of all. He was totally and absolutely committed to doing the will of His Father in everything so He bore it in faith. He did nothing of himself, but only as the Father had taught Him. In his own words "For I came down from heaven not to do my own will, but the will of him that sent me".

We are consistently informed in the gospels how Christ cast out demons and comforted everyone who came to Him for help. There were other sacrifices too, such as how He never married nor had children. He would never experience the joys and comfort of an earthly family. He traded ambition, wealth, prestige, position, popularity and other elements of success for the greater reward before Him. "For the joy that was set before Him, He endured the cross, despising the shame and has sat down at the right hand of the throne of God". (Hebrews 12:2). He considered His many fleshly sacrifices as nothing compared to the tremendous future He would enjoy in the Kingdom of God. Are we as concerned about our eternal state as our earthly position? Are we equally as concerned about God's will for our lives and for others, as opposed to our own fleshly desires? Paul the apostle teaches a great lesson in Philippians chapter three regarding the blessings related to true sacrifice. Using his own life as an example he outlines how he had everything a person could want, the right genes, the right social standing, the right education and reputation, yet he sacrificed it all for the sake of the gospel. Paul writes "But what things were gain to me, these I have counted loss for Christ. Yet indeed I also count all things as rubbish that I gain Christ and be found in him. That I may know him and the power of his resurrection and the fellowship of his sufferings being conformed to his death, if by any means I may attain the resurrection from the dead". (Philippians 3: 7-11). Paul instructs all of us to be like our Saviour Jesus Christ and be willing to sacrifice to "press toward the goal for the prize of the upward call of God in Christ Jesus". The glorious life of the Kingdom of God is only attained through sacrifice, but it will be worth it all in the end. Napoleon Hill states "Great achievement is usually born of sacrifice and is never the result of selfishness".

"Let go and let God" related to my own sacrifice regarding a ministry, children and a dog which had become so precious to me. I knew I must leave the children and Snowbell in Romania and trust God for their lives. I was conscious, that like every other sacrifice made for the benefit of others and for God Himself, the Lord has promised what we lose here on earth will be gained in the place called heaven. Jesus said "He that findeth his life shall lose it, and he that loses his life for my sake shall find it". (Matthew 10:39). Romania, more than anything else, has taught me that sacrifice is never easy; indeed it can be a most painful process, but there are times when it just has to be made. `

CHAPTER NINETEEN

HE WILL BE IN HEAVEN ONE DAY—WHAT ABOUT YOU?

"Verily, verily I say unto you, except a man is born again he cannot see the Kingdom of God" (John 3:3).

LESSON 19—ANIMALS WILL BE IN HEAVEN, YET MEN AND WOMEN WILL BE LOCKED OUTSIDE.

The fact that God used Snowbell to reveal so many of his own stunning qualities to me, made his loss even harder to accept. The lessons he taught me were endless. If Snowbell was a teacher of men then we would all learn to embrace our loved ones when they came home to us, be more impulsive and enjoy the journey of life, practice obedience, stretch before rising, on warm days stop to lie on your back on the grass and on hot days drink lots of water and snooze under a shady tree, never pretend to be someone you're not and delight in the simple joy of a long walk. On one such walk, having waved goodbye to our wonderful pet for the last time, I asked God a question, one that frankly I'd never asked before—will animals be in heaven? Whether or not people will see their pets again was a thought I hadn't honestly contemplated, having never previously owned one myself; yet suddenly it was all I could think about. I was not only confronted by this concept, but also challenged by it. Then my imagination exploded. Do animals have a soul? A spirit? How will they interact with man in heaven? Thankfully the Bible answered all of these questions for me in the affirmative in the years since. If you are a pet lover, how often have you also asked, will I see my pet again in heaven? Or will other animals be there? This is a perfectly natural question to ask, yet are you aware that God has always included the animals in Holy Scripture as part of the makeup of His wonderful Kingdom? Will your pet go to heaven? The good news is the Bible says many animals will be in heaven.

God's Word is surprisingly full of references to animals being in the Kingdom of God. For example, the book of Revelation points out that "All creatures recognise Jesus as the Saviour of the world and praise God right along with redeemed men" (Revelation 5:8-13). Isaiah too leaves us in no doubt about animals being in the Kingdom, stating "The wolf also shall dwell with the lamb, the leopard shall lie down with the young goat, the calf and the young lion and the fatling together and a little child shall lead them. The cow and the bear shall graze, the young ones shall lie down together; the nursing child shall play by a cobra's hole and the weaned child shall put his hand in the viper's den, they shall not hurt nor destroy in my holy mountain, says the Lord, for all the earth shall be full of the knowledge of the Lord as the waters cover the sea". One study on animals in the Kingdom reveals that the soul perceives, thinks, feels and makes decisions and choices. God gave man the choice to choose sin or righteousness, to worship himself or God. Significantly, the lesser animals were not given this choice. That's because God put them under the protection and dominion of man. In my absolute ignorance, when I was totally indifferent towards dogs and other animals, I used to think it didn't matter terribly about our attitude towards them. While I assumed we humans were given authority and dominion over the animals, I also clearly misunderstood this word dominion. When my wife and the children introduced me to Snowbell it was, with hindsight, the best thing that could have happened to me. I still needed to develop a strong love for animals and learn that they too are very much part of God's eternal Kingdom and heaven.

All of us have no doubt seen disturbing acts of cruelty towards animals— like the dog I mentioned in an earlier chapter, tied up for ten years. In my own country of Northern Ireland animal cruelty is still a problem. In the year 2012 a little dog by the name of Cody was torched with petrol by a gang of young people and set alight. The burns were so extensive that despite the best efforts of veterinarians to save him, the dog eventually had to be put to sleep. It was a disturbing story which exposed the cruelty of man. Clearly some treat their pets as their slaves and with extreme harshness, as evidenced by me in Romania, where horses, ponies and pigs were regularly beaten by their owners for no apparent reason. In parts of Europe in the year 2013 a slaughter house was discovered where horses had been killed in order to be used as meat products. This barbaric practice was instituted with absolutely no regard for an animal's welfare; rather for the purpose of increasing profits and to fool the public into thinking they were eating the best of beef. Thomas Edison once wrote "Until we stop hurting all other living beings, we are still savages". Thankfully such suffering by animals will not endure forever. Paul writes: "Because the creature itself also shall be delivered from the bondage of corruption, into the glorious liberty of the children of God. For we know the whole creation groaneth and travaileth in pain together until now" (Romans 8:21-22).

The word dominion simply means to "govern and control". True, God gave man control over his creature, but never the right to abuse that same creature. "A righteous man cares for the needs of his animal" says Proverbs (12:10). Paul also reminds us in Romans chapter eight that "though all creatures are subject to man's cruelty, God loves all His creation and has made plans for all his children and the lesser creatures to enjoy his eternal kingdom" (Romans 8:19).

The book of Job says of God's creation: "In whose hand is the soul of every living thing and the breath of all mankind". Even at the very beginning God made a covenant with man, saying "I will remember my covenant between me and you and all living creatures of every kind". This chapter also states: "The same fate awaits man and animals alike" (Genesis 9: 13-17). Animals are innocent, but let's not forget incredibly spiritual and sensitive to the world we live in.

How did Snowbell sense when I was about to go on holiday? How did he know when the storm was coming long before it set in? How did he distinguish between our children's bus and other buses if he couldn't see it, only hear it? Before the Asian tsunami on 26 December 2004, many of the animals had already left for the hills because they knew something dreadful was about to take place upon lower land. Just as well they did because shortly afterwards the worst tsunami in recent history occurred drowning and killing up to 230,000 people. The same thing happened in New York before the World Trade Centre disaster in 2001. The birds disappeared leaving the inhabitants of the city to face the full force of what is now known as 9/11. No wonder the patriarch Job wrote—"Ask the animals and they will teach you" (Job 12-7-10).

Even during the days of His flesh, the Lord Jesus walked in the wilderness where there were wild beasts and animals of various kinds. Incredibly many of the more volatile animals were restrained from touching Christ while God's purpose was fulfilled. What does this prove? You or I could not have walked near some of these dangerous creatures. Yet these animals were governed by the Spirit of God in exactly the same way as humans in order to fulfil God's plan for His Son's life.

It always amazed me how Snowbell would perceive something was wrong even before it took place. It was like a sixth sense. Prior to his departure to be with his new family he seemed very quiet and off colour. He knew well things were changing for him, yet don't ask me how. He would lie down and sulk and didn't eat much. His sad countenance confirmed he had identified something wasn't quite right. He would be leaving in a few days and he felt it in his bones. God's animals are truly remarkable creatures and they can teach us so much both about earthly things and heavenly things. When God considered destroying the world with a flood He found one man named Noah who, along with his family, was righteous before Him. God then decided to save Noah and his family, but interestingly he also saved at least one pair of every kind of animal, which identifies clearly God's love for the animal kingdom. If our Creator can fill an ark with animals and mankind to shelter them from the storm, how much more does He have the desire to populate heaven with people when Christ returns to the earth? In Revelation 19:11 we are reminded that "heaven was open and behold there was a white horse there". Imagine a white horse in heaven, yet even the horse will not be alone. God tells us: "Every animal of the forest is mine and the cattle on a thousand hills. I know every bird in the mountains and the creatures of the field are mine" (Psalm 50-10:11). In the book of Matthew Jesus said these words—"Are not two sparrows sold for a cent? And yet not one of them will fall to the ground apart from your

Father" (Matthew 10:29). Moreover, if our pets go to heaven, then doesn't it also make sense then that the owners will also have to go to heaven in order to see them there? Yet the reality is that while many pets and animals will be in heaven, men and women will be locked outside the gate. Maybe you haven't given any thought to this principle, but it's still something for you to consider carefully. Sadly the Bible makes it clear that the majority of people will not make it to heaven. Jesus said so himself: "Enter ye in at the strait gate; for wide is the gate, and broad is the way, that leads to destruction, and many there be which find it". (Matthew 7-13-17). I often think about this verse when I watch millions of people walking through the major cities of our world. All shapes, sizes and colours are merrily going about their daily business, but the Bible states that the majority of them will perish, why? Because they have not trusted in the Saviour, the Lord Jesus Christ, who is the only way to gain access to heaven. It is not possible to go there through our own good works or even through a religious experience or regular reciting of a creed. Paying tithes to the church won't help us reach God's eternal kingdom either. There is only one way to make it through the doors of God's glorious domain and that is through the blood of Jesus Christ, His Son. Jesus said "I am the way, the truth and the life, no man comes to the Father, except by me" (John 14:6). While later in the New Testament we are told "Neither is there salvation in any other, for there is none other name under heaven given among men whereby we must be saved" (Acts 4:12).

Still the Word of God reminds us that many will ultimately reject this great offer of salvation and yet God is just waiting mercifully for us to repent and confess our sins and if we do the Bible tells us that "He is faithful and just to forgive us our sins and to cleanse us from all unrighteousness" (2 John 1:9). He has already faithfully prepared a place for us in His kingdom; all we have to do is receive it. Consequently without reconciliation with God, the chances of seeing our departed pets again is nil and getting right with God is being born-again and adopted into the family of God. I was astonished at remarks I heard on a religious broadcast one Lord's Day which discussed the subject of heaven and who might be there. A well known religious scholar made the point that none of us really know who will be in heaven so, in effect, it is possible that all of us will be there. Yet the Bible is not only clear about who will be there, it is unequivocal about who won't be there. Jesus told Nicodemus "Verily, verily I say unto you, except a man is born again he cannot see the Kingdom of God" (John 3:3). Christ has told us in advance that those who will be in His Kingdom are those who are born again and those who will not be in His Kingdom are those who have not been born again. Our pass into heaven is therefore becoming part of God's wonderful adoption process. In the same way that Snowbell and the children we cared for in Romania found adopted families, how reassuring it is to know that God has also provided a way for all of us to be adopted into the family of God through the love of His Son at the cross. Paul writes in Ephesians "In love He has predestined us to be adopted as His sons through Jesus Christ in accordance with the pleasure of His will" (Ephesians 1 4-5).

When we first came across many of the children in Romania, they were rejected and neglected. They were orphaned and belonged to no one. Their natural parents had abandoned them and they literally had no family to be part of. However, when the children came to live with us, their material and spiritual needs were fully met. Their lives were restored and rebooted if you like and they became part of our family. So it is with Almighty God. We have become acceptable to God by being clothed with Christ. Orphaned by sin and left for dead, God makes us His own. He adopts us into his family. Through Christ we become His son and daughter and inherit eternal life in heaven. Adds Paul "For you have not received the spirit of bondage again to fear, but you have received the spirit of adoption whereby we cry, Abba father" (Romans 8:15). In our sinful state, none of us had any right to access the Kingdom of God, but having repented of sins and accepted Christ's offer of grace and mercy, in adopting us as His children, we can claim, even boast, to have found a home for all eternity.

No matter what tragedies have taken place in this world and there have been many of them, heaven is a place of tranquillity which God has promised to those that love and serve Him. It's a place where suffering and pain will be ended once and for all; a place where loved ones and yes, even our pets, will be reunited. So, if Snowbell and the rest of the animals will be in heaven one day—it's important not to close this book without asking the following question—what about you? Are you part of God's eternal and heavenly family yet? Have you given consideration as to whether or not you will make it to God's eternal destiny called heaven? His promise to anyone who gets right with Him is that they will enjoy eternal existence with Him and enjoy His creation forever in His kingdom and what a place heaven will be! It promises to be a place of reunion with our loved ones and our pets, a place of peace and serenity beyond our comprehension. It will be a place of no more night nor tears, no more separation or sorrow and no more death or pain, the like of which we constantly experience in this world. "And God shall wipe away all tears from their eyes and there shall be no more death, neither sorrow nor crying, neither shall there be any more pain, for the former things are passed away" (Revelation 21:4). Despite the sufferings in this temporal world, Paul tells us in the second book of Corinthians not to lose heart. He reminds us that though outwardly we are wasting away, inwardly we are being renewed every day. He says that light and momentary troubles are achieving for us an eternal glory that far outweighs them all, so we fix our eyes not on what is seen, but on what is unseen, since what is seen is temporary and what is unseen is eternal. Paul further points out that if the earthly tent we live in (which is our body), is destroyed; we have a building from God, an eternal house in heaven, not built by human hands. Think and dwell upon heaven, make it your focus for it is there we find our real and intended home. "The love of heaven makes one heavenly" said William Shakespeare adding "Words without thoughts never go to heaven".

Referring to the immensity of heaven and provision there, Jesus said "In my father's house are many mansions, if it were not so I would have told you, I go to prepare a place for you" (John 14:2). Isn't that more than words? Isn't that a most comforting thought? Christ, the King of Glory, has already prepared a place in eternity for those who have trusted Him as Saviour here on earth. And not just for His children, but for all of the animals too. Clearly what the Lord has prepared for us in His Kingdom is far beyond the imagination of us all. It's by far too great a concept for this writer to try and illuminate. But that's not to suggest that I don't have my own dreams and hopes of just what it will be like when one day I will meet up in heaven with Snowbell and many of our precious Romanian children there. For now, I am just grateful for the many magnificent lessons Snowbell taught me this side of eternity—the highest of all being "nothing beautiful in the world is ever really lost if we make it to God's Kingdom; for it's there where all things loved will undoubtedly live in our hearts forever"

EPILOGUE

S ow the seed and God will do the rest. With a mass of nations struggling both politically and economically these days, one could be forgiven for thinking that the future looks bleak. The pride of man accompanied by the desire for power has clearly twisted many governments, but that doesn't mean they can't recover. Five years after my exit from Romania I returned there in August 2013 and what I discovered encouraged me greatly and even gave me hope for the future.

I was curious to see if things had changed for the better and many questions still remained unanswered. How were the children doing whom we cared for at our children's home? Is God's Word still making an impact in Romania? How, too, are the people of this land coping compared to the "dark days" of Nicolae Ceausescu's ruthless regime, which hadn't petered out when both my wife Louise and I first arrived as missionaries in late 1999?

We had gone there, of course, to help an impoverished nation, to help the poor. God promised "He who is kind to the poor lends to the Lord and God will reward him for what he has done" (Proverbs 19:7). So I ventured back to see what God had done.

Once re-united with many of the children, they seemed happier than I'd anticipated, having matured into beautiful young men and women. Some are now at university, while others aspire to go there. Others are employed, both in Romania and abroad, and others are married having given birth to children of their own. What was apparent was just how much God had met their needs and taken care of many of them. Churches in Romania have been extended, too, while Christian schools which were in their infancy 15 years ago are now well developed providing spiritual education to the young people of this former Communist country. Don't get me wrong, Romania still requires oceans of love, support and financial help. Poverty is still very evident and brings to mind the words of Jesus—"the poor are with us always". Nevertheless I found it to be a very different place to the land I left behind in 2008. For example, there's much more international investment now, evident by the amount of High Street stores and food outlets we take for granted in the West. Numerous businesses have been initiated by young Romanian entrepreneurs and, for a nation once trapped in the grip of a brutal totalitarian system, such progress is most gratifying to observe. Child Protection measures have dramatically improved and children appear more secure than when we were resident in Romania. Even our much loved Labrador, Snowbell, is still being fed three times a day and massaged more than ever by his new family! He's a little older now, a little slower, but just as loveable as ever and in the best of hands. I'm reminded that if we sow the seed; God will do the rest. Paul wrote "I have planted, Apollos watered, but God gave the increase, so then neither is he that plants anything, neither he that waters, but God gives the increase" (1 Cor 3:6-7). The book of Ecclesiastes exhorts us to "Cast our bread upon the waters and after many days it will return unto you", (Ecclesiastes 11:1). In other words, our role as Christian workers is merely to "cast" "sow" and to "plant"; it's God who makes the real change and the real difference in struggling lives and in troubled nations like Romania.

After returning to my homeland I frequently worried about the welfare of Romania and its people, but following my excursion back there, it appears such fears may have proven unfounded. While this land has clearly much to do, work that may yet take generations, with God's help and the continued support of those dedicated to its development, signs are that Romania is heading in the right direction—and I'm so glad I got the opportunity to return and witness such growth for myself.